Good Home Cooking

Visit our How To website at www.howto.co.uk

At **www.howto.co.uk** you can engage in conversation with our authors – all of whom have 'been there and done that' in their specialist fields. You can get access to special offers and additional content, but most importantly you will be able to engage with, and become a part of, a wide and growing community of people just like yourself.

At **www.howto.co.uk** you'll be able to talk and share tips with people who have similar interests and are facing similar challenges in their lives. People who, just like you, have the desire to change their lives for the better – be it through moving to a new country, starting a new business, growing their own vegetables, or writing a novel.

At **www.howto.co.uk** you'll find the support and encouragement you need to help make your aspirations a reality.

You can go direct to www.good-home-cooking.co.uk, which is part of the main How To site.

How To Books strives to present authentic, inspiring, practical information in its books. Now, when you buy a title from **How To Books,** you get even more than just words on a page.

Make it, don't buy it! Enjoy real food at home

DIANA PEACOCK

Published by Spring Hill, an imprint of How To Books Ltd.
Spring Hill House, Spring Hill Road
Begbroke, Oxford OX5 1RX
United Kingdom
Tel: (01865) 375794
Fax: (01865) 379162
info@howtobooks.co.uk
www.howtobooks.co.uk

How To Books greatly reduce the carbon footprint of their books by sourcing their typesetting and printing in the UK.

The paper used for this book is FSC certified and totally chlorine-free. FSC (The Forest Stewardship Council) is an international network to promote responsible management of the world's forests.

British Library Cataloguing in Publication Data
A catalogue record of this book is available from the British Library.

ISBN: 978 1 905862 30 6

Produced for How To Books by Deer Park Productions, Tavistock, Devon
Designed and typeset by Mousemat Design Ltd
Edited by Jamie Ambrose
Printed and bound by in Great Britain by Ashford Colour Press Ltd, Gosport, Hants

Contents

This book is dedicated to our children, Rebecca, Joel and Joshua, and our daughter-in-law, Anouchka. They are all such grateful eaters and inspire my cooking.

Introduction

Good food is a right, not a luxury

Food is an important part of our lives – not simply because it keeps us alive, but because it gives us great pleasure. From the moment we are born, when most of our waking minutes are spent eating, to our very busy adult years, when we have to plan and shop for our food, eating should always be an enjoyable and satisfying experience. Too many times in today's hectic society, however, the thought of preparing our own food ends up feeling like a chore. The aim of this book is to change that feeling forever – by introducing you to the benefits and pleasures of good home cooking.

Everyone can have a go

We have come a long way from our parents' or grandparents' time, when the only convenience foods that existed were tins of meat or fish, or novelties such as canned soups. In contrast, we have modern luxuries such as microwaveable lasagne and boil-in-the-bag rice, yet I think we have actually missed out *because* of all these easy meals. We have forgotten our heritage of preparing and enjoying our own real food.

For this reason, I think it is important to re-learn some of the skills of our grandparents – and by this, I don't mean those of just our grand*mothers*. After all, it's not just the women in our families who are able to cook; my father and grandfather both enjoyed cooking and each had his own signature meals. Today, my husband is much better at making pastry than I am, and both of our sons are interested in making their own food and experimenting with flavours and ingredients.

All that aside, many of the recipes in this book are ones that both my daughter and I have developed together. We have made some terrible mistakes along the way (and still do!), but we have learned by them. It really is the only way.

This book enables you to make basic foods in the easiest and most convenient methods. We are more fortunate than our forebears in that we have labour-saving gadgets and more advanced ingredients that speed up the preparation of meals. My favourite example is fast-action yeast. These little sachets have halved the time and effort of bread-making, and the results are excellent and taste wonderful.

The most important message here is to have a go at a recipe. It won't necessarily be a total success the first or even the second time you try it, but I have discovered that the more you make your own food, the more you are certain that shop-bought meals are both inferior and also very expensive. If you keep at it, the day will come when you say to yourself, 'I could make that myself for half the price – and it will taste better.'

How do I go about it?

As the title says, this book was written to help you on your way to enjoying good home cooking. To start you off, the following tips are worth bearing in mind:

- Plan a few days' meals before going shopping. This prevents you from having to worry about what to make that night, when you're tired and hungry – and you won't spend as much money.

- When trying a new recipe, read it completely before you begin so you'll know the basic order of the method and have all your ingredients to hand. It's annoying to have to scrabble around at the back of cupboards looking for an ingredient, only to find, once you do have it, that it's out of date. (I've done this myself!)

- Create a store-cupboard so you're always ready to make basics such as pasta sauces, curries and cakes. The various chapters in this book will indicate the most useful basic ingredients to have to hand, but they will also teach you how to make some of your own ingredients such as pasta, pastry, cheese and even bacon.

- Have a go at dreaming up your own recipes by changing or adapting ingredients to suit your tastes. For example, if you don't like basil in one of my recipes, don't use it; try another herb that you do like, and if that doesn't work, try something else next time. You'll find a blank 'My Notes' page at the end of each chapter. Use this to write down any of your own recipe ideas, ingredients changes or other thoughts on the recipes you try so that you can refer to them in future.

- Taste as you go along. Personally, I don't like much salt, but I do like lots of pepper. Add just enough salt to give the right balance of taste to your dishes when preparing food. This will stop you and your family from showering food with salt before eating, and eventually you may not even need to put out the salt shaker on the table.

It may seem like a long way off now, but there will come a time when you'll be glad you are able to make your own food and not have to rely on meals prepared by people you don't know. Yes, it is a treat to buy easy-to-prepare foods or have a take-away; we do occasionally, and there's nothing wrong with that. But as you make more and more things yourself, the take-aways will become less and less frequent. You'll see that time can be found to cook your own food – because you *want* to do it, and so will your family and friends.

And just like you, they will all see that home-cooked food really is best.

Conversion Charts

Oven temperatures

°C	Gas mark	°F	Temperature
130	½	250	Very cool
140	1	275	Very cool
150	2	300	Cool
160/170	3	325	Warm
180	4	350	Moderate
190	5	375	Fairly hot
200	6	400	Fairly hot
210/220	7	425	Hot
230	8	450	Very hot
240	9	475	Very hot

Weight

Metric (approx.)	Imperial
25–30g	1oz
50–55g	2oz
85g	3oz
115g	4oz
140g	5oz
175g	6oz
200g	7oz
225g	8oz
250g	9oz
280g	10oz
350g	12oz
400g	14oz
450g	16oz/1lb
1kg	2lb 4oz

Liquid measure

Metric (approx.)	Imperial
25–30ml	1 fl oz
50ml	2 fl oz
75ml	3 fl oz
100–125ml	4 fl oz
150ml	5 fl oz
175ml	6 fl oz
200ml	7 fl oz
225ml	8 fl oz
250ml	9 fl oz
300ml	10 fl oz (½ pint)
600ml	20 fl oz (1 pint)
1 litre	1¾ pints

1

Making Your Own Dairy Products

Rather than buying all your dairy products from the supermarket, why not have a go at making your own? Given the amount of yoghurt we eat these days, it's always better to make your own because it is so much cheaper, it's better for the environment (no buying more plastic containers) and everyone can muck in and prepare their favourite flavours. In fact, yoghurt is probably the easiest of all the dairy products to make at home, because it is simply a matter of heating milk and introducing the bacteria that make the yoghurt.

Making cheese is also much easier than you think and it's great fun. And of course, people are always impressed when you tell them that what they're eating is homemade.

Making butter is always a riot in the kitchen, especially when the children do it. Our youngest son, Joshua, for instance, is an expert at knocking the fat out of cream to make butter; but then, he should be good at that, being a rugby player! You can have so much fun and although it isn't necessarily cheaper than shop-bought butter, it is always nicer. Besides, you couldn't get all that fun for the price of a 500g pack!

DAIRY PRODUCTS

Making Yoghurt

To make yoghurt, you have to introduce bacteria into the milk to thicken it and change the flavour. To do this you don't need any unusual ingredients – just milk and some unflavoured live yoghurt. Check the label and make sure there are no flavours, sweeteners or preservatives in the product. Alternatively, you can purchase a dried form of the probiotic starter bacteria, which comes in sachets, from smallholder suppliers. If you're going to make regular large quantities, this may give a more consistent result than just using ready-made natural yoghurt. Have a go at making it both ways and see which you prefer. Always follow the manufacturer's instructions on the packet when using the starter sachets.

You must use milk that has been unopened and is as fresh as possible. This makes sure that no other detrimental bacteria grow in the yoghurt. It takes around 6–8 hours for milk to become yoghurt, and it needs to be kept warm during this period. There are several ways of doing this:

- keep the pan in a constantly warm place, covered and wrapped in a tea cloth;
- pour the warm milk and starter into a large vacuum flask for the duration of the developing time; or
- buy a yoghurt maker that remains at a constant temperature – ideal for the job.

You will need some lidded containers for your finished yoghurt, especially if it is going to be taken in packed lunches. Otherwise, you can put the finished yoghurt in a large, covered container and keep it in the fridge for constant consumption.

Basic Yoghurt Recipe

This recipe makes just under 1kg of yoghurt.

1 litre fresh whole milk
3 tablespoons live natural yoghurt, at room temperature

1. Put the milk in a pan and bring to the boil.

2. Remove from the heat and allow to cool to 30°C.

3. Stir in the live yoghurt (known as the 'starter'), cover the pan and keep in a very warm place, or use a large vacuum flask.

4. The yoghurt should be ready after 6 hours. If it hasn't thickened sufficiently, leave it for another 2 hours.

5. When your yoghurt is ready, it may be eaten immediately or stored in a container in the fridge for 3–4 days.

6. It is best to flavour or sweeten the yoghurt just before you wish to eat it. This will keep it fresher for longer.

Serving suggestions

- Use in all recipes that require yoghurt, for topping your breakfast cereal or simply eating on its own.

- Sweeten the yoghurt with sugar or honey or add some freshly chopped fruit, dried fruit, chopped nuts or your favourite grains.

- Make a fruit compote by stewing fruit of your choice over a medium heat until it is tender; add sugar to taste if wished. This can then be stirred into the yoghurt. Purée the fruit if you prefer a smoother consistency.

Making Cheese

You can make most kinds of cheese in your home. Many kinds are complicated and time-consuming, so the recipes in this book are for the simplest cheeses that take very little time to make. Curd, cream and cottage cheeses are easiest and all require very little in the way of utensils.

How to make curds

To make most cheese, rennet is required. There are two types of rennet: vegetarian and rennet that is derived from calves' stomachs. Vegetarian rennet can be purchased from both supermarkets and smallholder suppliers, while the 'true' rennet can be purchased only from smallholder suppliers. Both contain the enzyme that forms the curds in the milk from which cheese is made. Curds are simply coagulated protein. Remember when using rennet always to read the manufacturer's instructions on the label for the correct quantity.

Other ingredients will have the same effect on milk as rennet, but to a lesser degree. Lemon juice and vinegar, for example, both curdle milk. Once the curds are rinsed, the flavours of vinegar and lemon juice disappear.

The cheese recipes on pages 8–10 use each of the three methods of forming curds. The utensils you will need to get started are:

- a large pan: one suitable for jam-making is ideal
- some cheesecloths or muslin bags
- a large sieve or fine colander
- a brewer's thermometer – obtained from a brewing or smallholding supplier
- a large bowl to contain the whey
- a long-bladed knife, such as a carving knife

DAIRY PRODUCTS

Curd Cheese

This is similar to an Indian paneer-type cheese.

3 litres whole milk
200ml natural yoghurt
3 tablespoons white vinegar
Salt to taste

1. Heat the milk in a large pan. Bring to the boil and stir in the yoghurt and vinegar. The curds will begin to form and separate from the whey, which is the liquid left over. This will taste of vinegar, so it cannot be used in baking.

2. Turn down the heat a little, and when the curds firm up, remove the pan from the heat.

3. Leave to cool for 10 minutes.

4. Line a colander with a cheesecloth and pour the curds and whey into the cloth. Hold the cloth steady as it will slip down and you may lose some of your curds – two pairs of hands are useful here.

5. Rinse under cold, gently running water, cutting into the curds with a knife. This will wash away any vinegar and unwanted whey.

6. Sprinkle the curds with a little salt (½–1 level teaspoon to taste) and cut into the curds to mix.

7. Gather up the ends of the cloth and tie securely, either together or with some cotton string.

8. Put the secured cheese back inside the colander and place over a bowl. To help the whey drain further, put a tin of food or some weights in a saucepan that fits on top of the cheese. This will act as a gentle press and force the whey out of the curds.

9. After 3–4 hours, carefully remove the cheese from the cloth and put into a dish.

10. Salt to taste and cut the salt into the curds to mix.

11. Using the back of a large spoon, press the curds down together to combine and form a good-shaped cheese. Sprinkle the top with a little more salt to help preserve it. Cover with greaseproof paper and store in the fridge. This cheese will keep for 5–6 days.

Simple Cottage Cheese

This is the easiest of cheeses to make and takes very little time. If you start it in the evening, it is ready to eat the day after. Jersey milk gives the best flavour for this – if you can get it.

1 litre whole milk
2 tablespoons lemon juice
Salt and pepper to taste

1. Heat the milk in a saucepan until just beginning to bubble, then remove from the heat.

2. Add the lemon juice and stir.

3. Pour into a bowl, cover and leave to stand overnight in a cool place, but not in the fridge, as this slows down the curdling process. (If you start it in the morning, leave it for at least 8 hours.)

4. In the morning, line a colander with a cheesecloth or muslin bag and pour the cheese into the colander over a bowl to collect the whey. This can be used for baking.

5. Rinse the bag of cheese under a slow-running cold tap and squeeze gently.

6. Hang the bag of cheese on a hook over a bowl and allow the whey to drip slowly for 4 hours. If you haven't a hook, tie a chopstick into the top of the cloth and rest the cloth over a bowl.

7. Once drained, put the cheese into a small bowl and add any seasoning you prefer. This will store in the fridge for 5 days.

Serving suggestion
Try one of the following ingredients to vary the flavour:

- chopped chives
- a little grated garlic and some fresh parsley
- sliced smoked salmon
- chopped black olives and an anchovy or two
- small chunks of chorizo
- a couple of chopped sun-dried tomatoes and a few fresh basil leaves

Cream Cheese

This is also a very easy cheese to make, but it requires a long waiting period before you can eat it. It is, however, well worth the effort.

800ml whole milk
700ml whipping cream
100ml crème fraîche
A few drops rennet; follow the instructions on the label for the exact amount

1. Put the milk and creams together in a large pan and gently whisk together over a very low heat.

2. Heat until the milk reaches 22°C, then remove from the heat.

3. Mix the rennet with a tablespoon of cool boiled water and stir into the milk in a figure-eight pattern.

4. Cover and leave to stand for 24 hours. After this time, the mixture should look like thick yoghurt.

5. Line a colander with a cheesecloth and pour in the milk mixture over a bowl to drain. The whey can be used for baking.

6. Bring up the ends of the cloth and either hang on a hook above a bowl or tie on a chopstick and rest over a clean container to catch the whey.

7. Leave to drip for 12 hours, or until the whey ceases to drip.

8. Remove the cloth and put the curds into a bowl. Using a wooden spoon, beat the curds gently until smooth and creamy.

9. Refrigerate for at least an hour before consuming to allow the flavours to develop.

Serving suggestion
Spread this on fresh bread, place in baked potatoes or team it with smoked salmon in a crisp roll. This cream cheese is ideal for use in dessert recipes and makes the best cheesecake I have ever eaten.

DAIRY PRODUCTS

How to Make Butter without a Churn

This recipe makes approximately 400g of butter.

1 x 2-litre plastic milk bottle and lid
1 litre of double cream, at room temperature
1 teaspoon salt, and more to taste

Have ready some small pots, either made of pottery or glass; clean and dry them well before use. Do not use plastic, as the fat content can dissolve the plastic and contaminate the butter. If the pots don't have lids, make a cover out of greaseproof paper tied with string.

1. Rinse the milk bottle in tepid water. Pour in the cream and secure the lid. The cream must not be too cold, and must be at least at room temperature. If it feels very cold, put the milk bottle under warm, not hot, running water for a few seconds.

2. Shake the bottle vigorously – an up-and-down motion is better than side-to-side. Keep going until you hear a change in the contents. When the butter appears, there is a thudding sound as the fat in the cream separates from the buttermilk.

3. Take off the lid and pour the buttermilk into a jug.

4. Cut round the widest part of the bottle and scoop out the butter. You will need to put this into a fine colander to rinse out the final dregs of buttermilk. This must be done, because it is the buttermilk that causes butter to sour prematurely. Clean the butter by running it under a slow, steady stream of cold water. Cut into it gently with a knife as you do so.

5. Add a teaspoon of salt, sprinkling it evenly over the butter. Cut it into the butter and keep rinsing. Do this for 4–5 minutes. The salt will be washed away in the liquid.

6. If you want unsalted butter, don't add any more salt. If you like it salted, add a level teaspoon of salt, put the butter on a clean chopping board and use the knife to mix the salt into the butter. More salt may be added in the same way if you like it really salty.

7. Press the butter into the clean, prepared pots, cover and store in the fridge. It will keep for 2–3 weeks. Your butter can now be used for spreading, frying and baking.

My Notes

2

Making Stock

Any chef will tell you that the secret to good food is good stock. It is the fundamental basis for all flavours, sauces, stews, soups and curries, and is guaranteed to drive you nuts with hunger during the cooking process. Whenever I make stock, Monty, our disreputable dog, sits on the kitchen doorstep and howls until we give him something to eat. A good stock makes you hungry: the best appetiser there is!

Whatever soup, casserole or meat sauce you're making, you will often reach for a stock cube to help the flavour of your dish. You can buy very expensive, ready-made stock and some high-quality stock cubes, but why not try making your own? Prepare a large batch and then freeze it in ice-cube trays or small containers until needed; see page 20 for storage information.

It is also economical to make your own as you can use leftovers that would normally be discarded. Scraps of meat and gristle, poultry carcasses and meat bones, vegetable peelings and trimmings can all be used when making stocks. You can buy meat bones cheaply from your butcher, but ask him to chop up the larger ones or they will never fit in your pan; the smaller the bones, the better the stock's flavour. Supermarkets sometimes have their own butcher, but if not, buy a joint of meat with the bone in, such as shoulder of lamb, ham or pork shanks or hocks. Beef bones are harder to come by in the supermarket as they are so big, so a trip to a butcher is necessary. Pig's feet are ideal for making stock, but they are difficult to find. Our local butcher said the reason he doesn't stock them is because there is no call for them. We buy ours from the big local outdoor market, but we have bought them in oriental supermarkets. If making fish stock, buy whole fish and use the heads, tails, skin and bones and cheaper cuts of fish such as coley or whiting. Do not use oily fish like mackerel or herring as the stock becomes greasy, and only used smoked fish if that's the flavour of the dish you are preparing, like kedgeree. The giblets inside a turkey or chicken add to the depth of your stock's flavour, but if you don't have them, don't worry.

Most stocks (except for fish) need long periods of cooking to produce the best flavour. Use a large, heavy-based pan with a tight-fitting lid. A pressure cooker will reduce the cooking time drastically. If using a pressure cooker, follow the manufacturer's guidelines for cooking this kind of food. Remember: the more you reduce the liquid in the stock, the more concentrated the flavour,

STOCK

Chicken and Poultry Stock

Any chicken or turkey leftovers: skin, bones, giblets, cooked or raw
About 3 litres of hot water
½ teaspoon each of dried thyme, parsley, sage and tarragon
1 teaspoon salt
White or black pepper to taste
1 large onion, sliced thickly
1 carrot, unpeeled and cut into large chunks
2 stalks and leaves of celery, chopped roughly

1. Put the meat scraps and bones in a pan (break up the carcass if necessary) and cover with the hot water. Stir in the herbs and seasoning.

2. Bring slowly to the boil, then turn down the heat and simmer gently with the lid partially on, for 1½ hours.

3. Remove the lid and add the vegetables. Replace the lid and continue to simmer gently for a further 1½ hours, checking that the water level doesn't drop too rapidly. If it does, add a little more.

4. Check the flavour for seasoning and adjust if necessary. If the flavour isn't strong, bring to the boil to evaporate some of the liquid. This will take about 15 minutes of boiling.

5. Skim off any white foam if you wish, but this is only protein so it doesn't spoil the flavour. Strain the stock into a large, clean bowl or pan; use a sieve rather than a colander, because the latter has bigger holes and will allow bits of bone and debris through.

6. Allow to cool completely. Remove any fat that has settled on the top if you want to reduce the calorific value of your stock.

Beef Stock

You'll get a much tastier stock if you roast the beef bones first. Because you won't want to make this every day, it's worthwhile spending a bit of time when you do in order to get the best-quality stock. It is time-consuming at first, but once it is simmering, it only requires a quick check every 30 minutes or so to see that it isn't boiling dry. This recipe makes plenty of stock – approximately 1½–2 litres – so have lots of containers ready to hold it. It is worthwhile getting marrowbones from a butcher and asking him to chop them into manageable pieces. Another useful tip is to keep any offcuts of beef you would normally throw away and freeze them for use when making stock (defrost before using). Don't worry if they are fatty; this will add to the flavour and will be skimmed off. This stock is *very* concentrated, so you not need to use much of it to flavour your dishes.

- Approximately 2kg marrowbones
- 2 onions, quartered
- 2 celery stalks, with leaves, sliced into 5–6 pieces, with chopped leaves
- 2 large carrots, chopped into 4–5 large chunks
- 2.5–3 litres of cold water: sufficient to cover the bones well
- 1 level teaspoon tomato purée
- 2 garlic cloves, peeled, optional
- ½ teaspoon dried mustard powder, optional
- 1 teaspoon dried parsley
- ½ teaspoon dried thyme
- 1 level teaspoon salt
- Black pepper to taste

1. In a large roasting tin, arrange the bones and any other scraps of meat you have saved. Add 1 of the onions, the celery and 1 carrot. Add about 300ml water and roast at 200°C/gas mark 6 for about 40–50 minutes, or until brown, not blackened, as this will cause the stock to have a bitter taste.

2. Have a large saucepan ready to take the bones and roasted vegetables. Put the contents of the roasting tin, including all the juices and bits on the bottom of the pan, into the saucepan and cover with water. Add the other vegetables, tomato purée, garlic and mustard powder, if using, and sprinkle in the herbs and salt and pepper. Give a stir and put on the heat; bring slowly to the boil. Once the stock is boiling, turn down the heat, partially cover the pan and simmer for 5 hours. Check the water levels off and on, topping up if it looks too low, but if it is simmering gently this shouldn't be necessary.

3. After the 5 hours of simmering time, bring to the boil and keep boiling for 10 minutes. Remove from the heat and carefully drain the stock through a sieve into a large bowl or pan. Take care: the bones and liquid are *very* hot.

4. Return the liquid to the original pan and boil for 10 minutes, or until reduced to your taste. If you're satisfied with the taste after draining, don't bother with this stage.

5. Allow to cool, skim any settled fat off the top, then pour into prepared containers for storing (see page 20).

STOCK

Fish Stock

When you're preparing fish, keep any trimmings and freeze them (unless previously frozen). This will allow you to avoid waste and bulk up the flavour of your fish stock. Try to avoid oily fish such as mackerel and herring. Some people also avoid salmon because it is slightly oily, but I think this a waste. Don't forget to use shellfish trimmings such as shells and heads, but avoid any intestinal parts, as the stock may become bitter. Adding dry white wine really enhances the flavour of finished fish stock, but it may be omitted if you wish. It is hard to say how much fish you will need; I use just as much as will fit comfortably in 1½ litres of water with the other ingredients.

- Fish trimmings and bits (see above)
- 1 leek, sliced roughly
- 1 carrot, quartered lengthways
- 2 celery sticks, chopped thickly
- 1.5 litres cold water
- 1 garlic clove (whole)
- 2 tablespoons fresh or 2 teaspoons dried parsley
- 2 bay leaves
- 2 level teaspoons salt
- Juice and zest of half a lemon
- 100ml dry white wine
- Black pepper to taste

1. Put all the fish bits and vegetables in a large pan and cover with the water.

2. Bring slowly to the boil. Add the other ingredients, turn down the heat and simmer gently for 45 minutes.

3. Strain the liquor carefully into a large bowl using a fine strainer – there may be some small bones wishing to escape.

4. For extra-concentrated flavour, return the stock to the pan and boil for 10 minutes.

5. Cool completely before either freezing in small containers (see page 20) or storing in a lidded jar for up to 3 days in the fridge.

Vegetable Stock

20g butter
2 leeks, cut into 2cm pieces
2 onions, sliced
3 celery sticks, chopped into small pieces
3 carrots, chopped
2 bay leaves
2–3 sprigs fresh thyme or 1 teaspoon dried
1 teaspoon dried parsley
5–6 crushed black peppercorns
1 teaspoon salt
2 litres water

1. Melt the butter in a large pan and add all the vegetables. Keep on a low heat, cover and sweat the vegetables for 20 minutes.

2. Add the herbs, peppercorns and salt and stir in the water.

3. Bring to the boil, then simmer for 35–40 minutes.

4. Strain and use, or store in a lidded container. Freeze as soon as it is cold.

Storing Your Stock

If you plan to use your stock fairly quickly, then it can simply be stored in the refrigerator. Chicken, meat and vegetable stocks will keep for 5–6 days in lidded containers in the fridge. Fish stock will keep for 3 days in the fridge.

By far the best way to store your stock is to prepare a large batch, allow it to cool thoroughly, then pour the cold liquid into ice-cube trays or small containers – but don't overfill, as otherwise it is tricky to put the trays in the freezer without spillage. If you're using ice-cube trays, two or three of these may be needed, or you can use a combination of trays and other, slightly larger containers. Make sure you label each type of stock, though, or you might end up using fish stock in a chicken soup!

Once frozen, your stock cubes can be used directly in dishes to enhance their flavour without even having to defrost them.

STOCK

My Notes

3

Soups, Snacks and Light Lunches

My husband said he couldn't believe that he had lived in the world for 50 years and had never tasted porcini mushrooms. Little does he know how inexpensive they are; he thought I had broken the bank! When you get to our age, the art of the light lunch pleases the waistline as much as the senses, but you do need to feel as though you have eaten something worth biting.

In this chapter, you'll learn how to make you own baked beans, potted sandwich fillings and savoury toasties – and every one of them is well worth a bite! But first, let me devote a few words to soup. Soup makes a wonderfully comforting meal. It can be offered either as a light lunch or as a filling main course. You can make a very tasty soup from simple vegetables. Accompanied by homemade bread, this creates a meal that is satisfying not just because it tastes so good, but also because of the pride you'll feel after having made something so wholesome.

SERVES 6–8

Ham and Vegetable Soup

You can buy a ham or pork shank for less than a couple of pounds. Ham shanks are saltier than a pork shank, so if you prefer a less salty dish, either soak the ham shank for 3 hours in cold water or use a pork shank; they taste equally good. Just look for one with the most meat around the bone.

- 1 ham or pork shank
- 1 large knob of butter
- 1 large onion, chopped
- 2 medium carrots, chopped
- 2 medium potatoes, peeled and diced
- 1 celery stick, chopped
- 1 small green pepper, chopped
- A handful of frozen green beans, chopped
- A handful of frozen peas
- Salt and pepper to taste
- 2–3 sprigs fresh thyme or ½ teaspoon dried
- 1 tablespoon chopped fresh parsley or 1 level teaspoon dried

1. Cook the shank in a large pan with sufficient water to cover well and bring to the boil; add a little salt if it is pork. After boiling point is reached, turn down the heat and cover and simmer gently for 2½ hours.

2. Remove from the heat after the cooking time and lift out the joint. Leave it on a plate to cool – it will be used later.

3. Pour the stock liquid into a large bowl and conserve.

4. Add a knob of butter to the pan and melt gently over a low heat.

5. Add all the vegetables, seasoning to taste, and if you are using dried herbs add these also. Stir well so that the ingredients are coated in butter.

6. Cover and allow the vegetables to 'sweat' for 15–20 minutes. This very gentle initial cooking extracts the full flavour of all the vegetables before any liquid is added.

7. Stir and add the liquid from the meat. If using fresh herbs, add them at this stage. If there isn't enough liquid to cook the soup, add a little more hot water to make about 2 litres. The liquid measurement is very approximate; just make sure there is enough to cover the vegetables with about 3cm spare. You can always top up with water if necessary during the cooking time.

8. Bring to the boil, then turn down the heat and simmer for 40 minutes. Check and adjust the seasoning during this time.

9. While the soup is cooking, remove all the meat from the bones, chop it into bite-size pieces and add to the soup once the 40 minutes are up. Stir well and cook for 10 more minutes.

10. Soup tastes best if it is allowed to stand for 15–20 minutes before serving; this allows the flavours to develop. It can then be reheated and served. If you have any left over, allow to cool and either store in the fridge for 48 hours or pour into a freezeable container, label and store frozen for up to 2 months.

SERVES 4–6

Minestrone-style Soup

This recipe is based on Italian minestrone soup – but it is a quicker version.

4 rashers streaky bacon, sliced into small strips
1 tablespoon sunflower or vegetable oil
1 medium onion, chopped finely
2 carrots, diced into small cubes
1 celery stick, chopped
1 green pepper, diced
A handful of frozen green beans, defrosted and sliced into 1cm lengths
2 garlic cloves
½ teaspoon dried marjoram or oregano
500ml passata or 400g canned chopped tomatoes
1 litre vegetable or chicken stock (see pages 19 and 16)
150g dried small pasta shapes
200g canned cannellini beans

1. In a large saucepan, fry the bacon gently and add the oil.

2. Add all the fresh and frozen vegetables, and cook them gently with the bacon over a low heat for 10 minutes

3. Stir in the garlic, herbs and passata or canned tomatoes.

4. Add the stock and bring to the boil, then turn down the heat and simmer for 30 minutes.

5. Stir in the pasta and cook for 10 minutes.

6. Add the cannellini beans and cook for 5 minutes. Sprinkle with a little of your favourite cheese and serve with some crusty bread.

Storage

Any leftover soup will keep in the fridge for 2–3 days and freeze for up to 2 months.

SERVES 4–6

Cream of Tomato Soup

This is a real family favourite and tastes delicious served immediately. Although it is freezeable, it somehow doesn't taste as good as when it is freshly made, so it is best eaten on the same day.

- 30g butter
- 1 medium onion, chopped finely
- 1 garlic clove, crushed
- 2 tablespoons tomato purée
- 1 teaspoon paprika
- 800g fresh, ripe tomatoes, chopped roughly
- 650ml vegetable stock (see page 19)
- A pinch grated nutmeg
- 2 teaspoons sugar
- Salt and pepper to taste
- 1 tablespoon chopped fresh parsley
- 100ml double cream

1. Melt the butter in a saucepan and fry the onions gently until they are translucent (but not brown).

2. Add the garlic, tomato purée, paprika and the tomatoes, stir and cook gently for 10 minutes.

3. Add the stock, nutmeg, sugar and any seasoning and bring to the boil.

4. Stir in the parsley and simmer for 25 minutes.

5. Either use a hand blender to purée the soup in the pan or pour it into a food processor and process in batches. If you do not have a blender or processor, push the soup through a sieve.

6. Return the soup to the pan and stir in the cream. Reheat the soup until it is hot; do not boil, as this will impair the flavour. Serve immediately with an extra swirl of cream and a little sprinkling of parsley.

SERVES 4

Mushroom Soup

This is the quickest soup to make from scratch and it's good to serve on special occasions. It can be made earlier in the day and then reheated gently before serving. Use a combination of medium-sized closed-cup and large open-cup mushrooms; this gives you the best flavour and colour. If you use all open-cup ones, the finished soup is a dark, murky grey, but they have the strongest flavour. I like plenty of black pepper in mushroom soup, but this is up to you.

250g mushrooms, chopped
50g butter
Approximately 350ml milk, at room temperature
1 tablespoon plain flour
Salt and black pepper to taste
4 tablespoons single cream

1. Fry the mushrooms gently in half of the butter until just soft.

2. Strain the liquor into a measuring jug and make up to 450ml by adding the milk.

3. Set aside the cooked mushrooms and melt the rest of the butter on a low heat in a saucepan.

4. Stir in the flour with a wooden spoon and gradually add the milk mixture a little at a time. Raise the heat slightly and bring to the boil, stirring constantly.

5. Turn down the heat and simmer gently while adding the mushrooms and season to taste.

6. Simmer for 2–3 minutes and add the single cream. Serve immediately with some thin slices of raw mushroom on top.

SERVES 4

Leslie's Potato Soup

This was always my favourite soup as a child; it was my dad's speciality. It is delicious on a cold day, but very filling.

200ml milk
1 bay leaf
100g butter
1 medium onion, chopped finely
450g potatoes, cubed
500ml vegetable or chicken stock (see pages 19 and 16)
Salt and pepper
Chopped chives or toasted breadcrumbs, for sprinkling

1. Heat the milk to just boiling and pour over the bay leaf in a heatproof jug. Leave to steep while preparing the vegetables.

2. In a heavy-based saucepan, melt the butter. Add the onions and fry gently until they are translucent.

3. Add the potatoes and stir into the butter. Cook gently for 2–3 minutes, then add the stock and season well to taste.

4. Bring to the boil, then simmer for 10 minutes.

5. Remove the bay leaf from the milk, pour the milk into the soup pan and stir.

6. Simmer the soup for another 10 minutes, or until the potatoes 'fall' (break apart) into the soup.

7. Remove from the heat and mash the last bits of potato, or hand-blend to make a smooth consistency. Serve garnished with chopped chives or toasted breadcrumbs.

SERVES 4–6

Vegetable Soup with Herb Dumplings

Dumplings turn a soup into a hearty meal. They can be made very easily and dropped into a soup during the last 20 minutes of cooking, but note that they are not really suitable for creamy soups that cannot be simmered vigorously at the end.

For the soup

1kg vegetables: a mix of carrots, green beans, cauliflower, broccoli, peas, courgettes or anything else you wish to use up
2 small potatoes
1 celery stick
1 large onion
2 tablespoons butter
½ teaspoon dried thyme
1.5 litres vegetable stock (see page 19)

For the dumplings

100g self-raising flour
Pinch salt
50g vegetarian suet
Pepper to taste
Pinch each of dried thyme, sage, rosemary and tarragon
About 4 tablespoons water to mix

1. Cut all the vegetables into small pieces.

2. Heat the butter in a large pan and fry the onion for a few minutes.

3. Add all the vegetables and thyme, cover the pan and sweat the vegetables gently for 15 minutes.

4. Add the stock and bring to the boil.

5. Turn down the heat and simmer the soup for 40 minutes.

6. Meanwhile, make the dumplings. Sift the flour and salt together and stir in the suet, seasoning and herbs. Mix in the water to make a soft but not too sticky dough. If the mixture is too sticky, simply sprinkle a little more flour over the dough and work it in lightly with your fingertips. Roll the dough into 12 small balls.

7. After the 40 minutes of cooking time is up, make sure the soup is simmering vigorously and drop in the dumplings as quickly as you can. Replace the lid and leave for 15 minutes.

8. Serve immediately. This will keep covered in the fridge for 2–3 days.

SERVES 4–6

Chicken Soup

This soup is traditionally thought to aid recovery after a heavy cold or influenza, and science has since proven that chicken soup does have beneficial effects. This recipe certainly makes you feel better. To get the real benefit from the chicken, leave the skin on and cook unboned.

- 2 chicken thighs
- 2 chicken drumsticks
- Salt and black pepper to taste
- 2 litres water or chicken stock (see page 16) or a combination of both
- A knob of butter
- 1 large onion, chopped finely
- 2 large or 3 medium carrots, chopped
- 2 celery sticks, chopped into 1cm pieces
- 1 garlic clove, crushed or chopped
- ½ teaspoon each of dried thyme, tarragon and marjoram, or 1 teaspoon dried herbes de Provence
- 3 tablespoons long-grain rice
- 1 tablespoon fresh parsley, chopped

1. Put the chicken pieces in a large pan and season with a little salt and pepper. Pour over half of the water or stock and bring to the boil. Cook at boiling point for 2–3 minutes, then turn down the heat and simmer for 40 minutes.

2. Strain the chicken pieces, reserving the liquor in a heatproof bowl or jug and putting the chicken on a plate.

3. In the same pan, melt the butter and fry the onion until translucent.

4. Add the carrot, celery, garlic and herbs (excluding the parsley). Turn down the heat, cover and sweat the vegetables together for 10 minutes.

5. Meanwhile, strip all the meat from the chicken pieces, ready to add to the soup.

6. Pour the liquor from the chicken and the rest of the stock or water into the saucepan. Check the seasoning and bring to the boil.

7. Add the rice and simmer for 15 minutes.

8. Stir in the chicken and fresh parsley. Simmer for 5 minutes, then serve.

Storage
This soup will keep in the fridge for 2–3 days, or freeze for 2 months.

SERVES 4 AS A MAIN COURSE, OR 6 AS A STARTER

Seafood Soup

This is a seafood-lover's soup. It makes an excellent starter course at a special dinner, or is a wholesome meal on its own when served with some homemade crusty bread.

600ml milk
200g haddock
200g whiting or other white fish
Salt and black pepper to taste
Pinch grated nutmeg
1 tablespoon butter
1 medium onion, chopped finely
2 garlic cloves, chopped
1 tablespoon plain flour
600ml fish stock (see page 18) or water
2 tablespoons lemon juice
½ small glass of dry white wine
300g cooked, peeled prawns, defrosted if frozen
100g mussels
1 tablespoon chopped fresh parsley
4 tablespoons single cream

1. Poach the haddock and other white fish in the milk for 5 minutes with some salt and black pepper and the nutmeg.

2. Strain the fish, retaining the milk. Flake the fish and check for any bones.

3. In a large pan, melt the butter and fry the onion gently, without browning, until they are soft. Add the garlic and stir.

4. Remove from the heat and stir in the flour. Place back on the heat and gradually add the poaching milk and the stock or water, stirring with a wooden spoon until all the liquid is combined with the flour mixture.

5. Add the lemon juice and wine; stir these in vigorously. Raise the heat to bring the soup to boiling point, then turn down to a low simmer. Check the seasoning and adjust if necessary.

6. Add the flaked fish, prawns, mussels and half of the parsley. Simmer for 5 minutes. Stir in the cream and serve garnished with the rest of the parsley.

SERVES 4

Lentil and Bacon Soup

- 4 rashers back bacon
- 2 rashers streaky bacon
- A little oil for frying
- 1 medium onion, chopped finely
- 1 garlic clove, chopped
- 2 carrots, chopped
- 1 dessertspoon tomato purée
- ½ teaspoon celery salt
- 1.5 litres vegetable stock (see page 19)
- 5 tablespoons lentils
- Salt and pepper to taste

1. Fry the bacon in the oil until cooked and add the onion, garlic and carrot. Cook on a low heat for 10 minutes.

2. Stir in the tomato purée and celery salt.

3. Gradually add the stock and then stir in the lentils.

4. Bring to the boil, stirring continuously as the lentils can rest on the bottom of the pan and stick.

5. Turn down the heat to simmering and cook for 40 minutes, stirring occasionally.

6. Check the seasoning – black pepper really enhances the flavour of this soup – and serve immediately.

Storage
Store in the fridge for 2–3 days. This soup freezes for up to 2 months.

TOASTIES AND TOAST TOPPERS

These quick and simple recipes make a light lunch feel special – especially on those days when a cold sandwich just will not do. You can use any kind of bread, from wholemeal to French batons – whatever you fancy.

The following recipes are sufficient for 2 large pieces of toast, so would serve 2 people unless otherwise indicated.

Easy Welsh Rarebit

This isn't really Welsh Rarebit, but it is just as delicious. Grate more or less cheese if you wish; the amount below is only approximate.

1 egg yolk
½ teaspoon wholegrain mustard
4 tablespoons double cream
150g mature Cheddar, grated

1. Beat the egg yolk and mustard into the cream and mix into the cheese.

2. Spread onto freshly toasted bread, keeping away from the edge as it will spread under the grill.

3. Place under a hot grill until the cheese melts and browns.
Serve immediately.

TOASTIES AND TOAST TOPPERS

Mackerel and Soft Cheese

This is a rich topping that is a must for mackerel-lovers to try.

2 x 125g cans mackerel, either in oil or brine, drained well
8 peppercorns, roughly crushed
1x 150g tub light soft cream cheese

1. Flake the mackerel and mash it well with a fork.

2. Stir in the black pepper and beat in the cream cheese.

3. Toast your bread. Butter it if you wish and spread the mackerel mixture very thickly on top.

4. Serve immediately with slices of fresh tomato dressed with a dash of balsamic vinegar.

Bacon, Beef Tomato and Brie

1 beef tomato, sliced thickly
A sprinkling of balsamic vinegar
4 rashers back bacon, grilled
4 wedges Brie

1. Put the slices of tomato on a plate and sprinkle with a little balsamic vinegar.

2. Toast your bread and butter it if you wish. Place the bacon on top. Add a slice of tomato and finish with a wedge of Brie.

3. Grill until the Brie melts and serve immediately.

SERVES 6–8

Homemade Baked Beans

Peel the tomatoes if you wish by dipping them first into boiling water, then into iced water. They will peel easily. But the beans taste good with the skins used as it gives the finished dish greater depth of flavour. If they are chopped up well you'll hardly notice the skins.

- 500g haricot beans, soaked in cold water overnight, then drained
- 2 red onions, finely chopped
- 1 tablespoon olive oil
- 12 ripe tomatoes, chopped
- 4 level teaspoons unrefined sugar
- 200ml passata
- Salt and pepper to taste

1. Cook the beans in a pan with just enough hot water to cover them. Bring to the boil, then simmer for 20 minutes. Drain well.

2. In a separate saucepan, fry the onions gently in the oil until just tender, then place in an ovenproof lidded casserole.

3. Stir in the chopped tomatoes, sugar, passata and beans. Season with salt and pepper.

4. Preheat the oven to 165°C/gas mark 3.

5. Stir well, cover the casserole and place in the oven for 30 minutes. Stir, then cook for another 30 minutes. Check that the beans are tender; if not, cook them for a further 15 minutes.

6. These taste better if they are allowed to cool slightly before serving. Cool completely before storing.

7. Serve on hot buttered toast. They taste good with some ground white pepper sprinkled on the top.

Storage

This makes more than a two-portion serving, but it is worth making as they keep well in jars with secure lids in the fridge, or they can be frozen in lidded containers.

Caramelised Tomatoes and Cheddar

6 ripe tomatoes, sliced thinly
½ level teaspoon soft brown sugar
A little sunflower oil, for drizzling over the tomatoes
About 150g grated Cheddar

1. Preheat the oven to 200°C/gas mark 6. Place the tomatoes on an oiled baking sheet and sprinkle the sugar over the top.

2. Drizzle with oil and place in the oven for 25 minutes, or until the tomatoes have started to caramelise. Turn the heat up to 225°C/gas mark 7 and cook for 5 minutes more.

3. Toast your bread and butter. Spread the tomatoes evenly over your toast and sprinkle with the grated Cheddar.

4. Grill until the cheese melts and serve immediately.

Creamed Mushrooms

You can use any type of mushrooms for this recipe. If they are different sizes, slice the very big ones so that they cook at a similar rate to the smaller ones; otherwise some will be overcooked.

A knob of butter
200g mushrooms
4 tablespoons double cream
2 tablespoons crème fraîche
Salt and coarsely ground black pepper to taste

1. Melt the butter in a frying pan and fry the mushrooms until tender.

2. Add the cream and crème fraîche, and season with salt and pepper.

3. Serve on hot buttered toast.

Serving suggestion
This is also delicious if you chop a few rashers of bacon and fry them until crisp, then add your mushrooms and continue to follow the recipe.

TOASTIES AND TOAST TOPPERS

Joshua's Pizza Toasties

This is my son Joshua's recipe. He makes these with whatever we have in the fridge, but you always need tomato purée and some sort of cheese. You can use french batons, large slices of bread or baps sliced in half.

- 4 slices bread or a baton cut in half lengthways
- 3 tablespoons tomato purée mixed with 1 tablespoon of olive oil, a crushed garlic clove and a tablespoon of water
- Either 185g canned tuna, drained well, or some chopped cooked ham or chicken
- Sufficient grated cheese to cover each slice of toast very generously: mozzarella, red Leicester or Cheddar are good cheeses to use, either individually or combined

1. Lightly toast the bread and spread with the purée mixture.

2. Pile on the tuna, ham or chicken and sprinkle with the cheese.

3. Place on a baking sheet and put in the top or the hottest part of your oven at 225°C/gas mark 7 until the cheese begins to bubble.

4. Serve immediately.

SERVES 2

Pizza Cobs

These are made with those round, crusty cob rolls – and if they have gone a bit stale, all the better: they're just as good and you don't have to throw them away. One cob per person is usually sufficient.

- 2 large, crusty cobs
- 2–3 tablespoons olive oil
- 3 tablespoons sun-dried tomato purée, mixed with 2 tablespoons water
- 2 ripe tomatoes
- 100g Cheddar, cubed
- 2 anchovies
- 6 pitted black olives, halved
- 100g mozzarella, chopped

1. Preheat the oven to 200°C/gas mark 6. Cut the top off each cob, about 1cm down the side. Pinch out some of the centre of the cob, then press well down in the centre to make a hollow.

2. Drizzle some of the olive oil inside the cob. Spread the tomato purée mixture evenly over the inside.

3. Layer slices of tomato, some cubes of Cheddar, another slice of tomato, an anchovy and the halved black olives. Drizzle a little more olive oil over the contents and top with mozzarella.

4. Put the lid on, squashing the filling into the cob.

5. Wrap each cob in foil and put on a baking sheet. Bake in the preheated oven for 20–25 minutes.

Serving suggestion

These are wonderful cut in half vertically and served with a green salad.

SERVES 4

Potato Cakes

These are great for breakfast, lunch or any time. Next time you serve mashed potatoes with a main meal, use any leftovers to make these cakes.

- 450g potatoes suitable for mashing; peeled and cut into equal-sized chunks
- 50g butter
- Salt and pepper to taste
- 100g plain flour
- Oil for greasing

1. Boil the potatoes in salted water until tender. Drain well in a colander and put back in the warm pan to dry out.

2. Add the butter and season to taste with salt and pepper. Mash well until smooth.

3. Sift half the flour into the potato and mix with your hands to make a pliable dough. Add more flour until this consistency is achieved.

4. Either roll out the whole of the dough to 2cm deep and cut out rounds with pastry cutters, or use a food ring to form the cakes.

5. Rub or spray a very small quantity of oil onto a griddle or flat-based frying pan. Place on a medium heat and fry each cake on both sides for 3 minutes, or until they brown.

6. Serve hot, or allow to cool and serve within 24 hours.

Serving suggestion
Try serving them topped with a soft poached egg and crispy bacon, or some smoked salmon and scrambled eggs.

SERVES 4

Porcini Mushrooms

These are delicious served with the potato cakes on page 39. They are also easy to cook on a barbecue if you want something different.

80g minced pork
25g breadcrumbs, made by grating a stale crust of bread
1 garlic clove, chopped
Salt and black pepper to taste
4 large porcini mushrooms
40g mozzarella cheese, chopped

1. In a bowl, combine the pork, breadcrumbs, garlic and seasoning.

2. Remove the stalk from the mushrooms, setting aside the caps. Chop the stalks roughly and add them to the pork mixture.

3. Stuff each mushroom cap with an equal amount of the pork mixture and top with some mozzarella.

4. Either place on an oiled baking sheet and cook at 200°C/gas mark 6 for 15–20 minutes, or place on the barbecue and cook until the cheese bubbles and the pork is cooked.

POTTED MEATS AND FISH

Making your own potted meat sandwich fillers is both easy and economical because you use up your cooked meats and make them go further. You also know exactly what goes into them.

A food processor is necessary to get the very smooth texture of the finished commercial product, and it just makes things easier and quicker, but if you don't have one, chopping the meat until it is very fine and mashing in the other ingredients will yield a similar, if less smooth, finish. When topping potted meat or fish with melted butter, make sure that the butter has cooled slightly first; otherwise any heat may spoil the contents underneath.

Potted Chicken

250g cooked chicken
50g butter
A pinch of grated nutmeg
A pinch of cayenne pepper
Half a garlic clove, chopped finely
2 teaspoons lemon juice
Salt and pepper to taste
50g melted butter

1. Put all the ingredients except the melted butter into a food processor and blend to a rough paste.

2. Pack into clean containers – ramekins are ideal for this – and pour the melted butter on top of each. This seals in the potted chicken and keeps it fresher for longer.

Storage
This will keep for 2–3 days in the fridge.

POTTED MEATS AND FISH

Potted Beef

250g cooked beef, free of gristle and fatty bits
50g butter
½ teaspoon English mustard
A dash of Worcestershire sauce
Salt and pepper to taste
50g melted butter

1. Put all the ingredients except the melted butter into a food processor and blend to a rough paste.

2. Pack into containers and pour the melted butter on top of each. This will keep for 2–3 days in the fridge.

Serving suggestion
For a special occasion, add a tablespoon of port to the ingredients before they are processed.

Potted Smoked Mackerel

If you are going to serve this immediately, omit the topping of melted butter. Instead, just sprinkle a little fresh parsley on top or add a fine sliver of lemon.

250–280g smoked mackerel, skinned and boned
80g butter
1 tablespoon chopped fresh parsley
1 small spring onion, chopped
Juice of 1 lemon
Salt and pepper to taste
50g melted butter

1. Put all the ingredients except the melted butter into a food processor and blend to a paste.

2. Put into containers and pour the melted butter on top of each to seal.

Storage
This will keep for 4–5 days in the fridge.

POTTED MEATS AND FISH

Potted Salmon

200g salmon fillets
50g butter, softened
1 tablespoon
double cream
A little grated nutmeg
Salt and black pepper

1. Steam or oven-bake the salmon until it is just cooked through. Allow to cool completely.

2. Flake the fish in a bowl and add all the other ingredients. Use a fork to mash everything together.

3. Put into ramekins and put a disc of baking or greaseproof paper on top of each to seal. Store in the fridge and consume within 3 days.

Serving suggestion
Try adding a teaspoon of chopped dill to the ingredients for variety.

Potted Shrimp or Prawns

You can buy brown shrimp from fish markets, but if you can't get hold of them use fresh or defrosted and drained prawns.

250g precooked brown
shrimp or prawns
Salt and black pepper
to taste
80g melted butter
¼ teaspoon
cayenne pepper

1. Force as many prawns or shrimp as will fit into ramekin dishes and season with salt and black pepper.

2. While the butter is melting, add the cayenne pepper and stir to mix thoroughly.

3. Pour the butter over the shrimp or prawns and allow to set before serving with hot toast. The butter from the prawns will melt into your toast. Delicious!

SANDWICH FILLERS

Ideas for sandwiches can begin and end with slices of ham or cheese. Although these are sometimes just what you fancy, it is good to have a few other ideas in your repertoire – especially when you're making packed lunches.

Coronation Chicken

This can be made the night before preparing packed lunches.

A knob of butter
Half a red onion, chopped finely
200–250g cooked chicken, chopped
5 dried apricots, chopped
3 tablespoons mayonnaise mixed with 1 rounded teaspoon mild curry powder
1 tablespoon double cream

1. Melt the butter in a saucepan and sauté the onion gently until translucent. Allow to cool.

2. In a bowl, combine all the ingredients, including the cooked onions, and mix well.

Savoury Cheese and Carrot

150g grated mature Cheddar
1 medium carrot, grated
2 tablespoons mayonnaise
2 teaspoons chopped chives
Black pepper to taste

1. Combine all the ingredients in a bowl and spread onto your bread. This may also be prepared the day before you want to use it.

Spicy Prawn Mayonnaise

200g precooked prawns
3 tablespoons mayonnaise
½ teaspoon paprika
¼ teaspoon cayenne pepper
1 teaspoon sweet chilli sauce

1. Put the prawns in a bowl and mix in all the other ingredients until fully combined. This one is best consumed immediately.

My Notes

4

Cooking with Cheaper Cuts of Meat and Fish

'It's not exactly a T-bone, is it?' That was my son's reaction when he looked at the parcel from the butchers, but in the end even he had to admit that it tasted wonderful after being treated to a long, slow simmer in the oven.

Which just goes to show that good food doesn't have to be expensive. The art of creating wonderful meals from cheap cuts of meat is something my mother, and my grandmother before her, excelled at. It's about time that we, too, began to realise that good food doesn't have to be expensive!

SERVES 6–8

Roasted Brisket with Root Vegetables

This is a comforting dish that takes very little in the way of preparation. It can be put in an ovenproof casserole and left in the oven until ready for serving, perhaps with a green vegetable. Look for the leanest cut of meat. This can be difficult, as brisket is usually rolled and tied, but check the depth of the lean layers – the deeper the better.

A brisket joint, about 1.5–2kg in weight
About 600ml water
Salt and pepper to taste
1 tablespoon flour or gravy powder
½ teaspoon mustard powder
4 carrots, scrubbed and chopped into large chunks
2 medium parsnips, peeled and sliced
Half a medium swede, peeled and chopped into chunks
2 small turnips, peeled and chopped into chunks
A couple of sprigs fresh thyme or 1 level teaspoon dried

1. Preheat the oven to 180°C/gas mark 4.

2. Place the meat in an ovenproof casserole or roasting pot and add sufficient water to come a third of the way up the meat. Season the top of the meat and put into the preheated oven.

3. Cook for 1 hour, then lift out of the oven. Mix the flour or gravy powder and the mustard with a little cold water to make a paste and stir into the water around the meat.

4. Arrange the vegetables and herbs around the meat, season to taste and put back in the oven. Turn the oven down to 170°C/gas mark 3 and cook for 2½ hours, or until the meat and vegetables are tender.

5. Lift the meat out of the pot and allow it to rest for 10 minutes before carving. The vegetables may be kept warm in the oven.

6. Serve the meat with the vegetables and gravy.

Serving suggestion

This goes well with some slow-roasted potatoes. Peel 4–6 potatoes and cut them into chunks, slightly smaller than you would when normally roasting potatoes. Place on an oiled baking sheet and coat with the oil. Season and cook these with the meat at the top of the oven about 1½ hours before meat is cooked. Alternatively, put the potatoes around the meat with the other vegetables and it becomes a one-pot meal.

SERVES 6

Beef and Vegetable Cobbler

This makes a change from a pastry-topped dish.

oil for frying
1 large onion, sliced
450g stewing beef
1 tablespoon flour
3 medium carrots, scrubbed and sliced into discs
Half a small squash, diced
2 medium leeks
2 large potatoes
2 celery sticks
2 tablespoons chopped fresh parsley or 1 teaspoon dried
2 tablespoons tomato purée
350ml water or beef or vegetable stock (see pages 17 and 19)
Salt and pepper

For the cobbler

180g self-raising flour
Salt and black pepper to taste
½ level teaspoon of cayenne pepper
60g Cheddar
30g butter
1 egg
5 tablespoons milk

1. Heat the oil in a saucepan and fry the onion until soft. Transfer to an ovenproof dish.

2. Fry the meat in the same pan until it is just brown. Sprinkle with the flour and add to the onions.

3. Add the vegetables and parsley and stir to combine.

4. Stir the tomato purée into the stock and pour this over the meat and vegetables.

5. Cover and cook for about 1½ hours at 190°C/gas mark 5.

6. Meanwhile, make the cobbler. Sift the flour, salt and cayenne pepper into a mixing bowl and rub in the butter. Stir in a little black pepper and the Cheddar.

7. Beat the egg and milk together and mix into the dry ingredients.

8. Use your hands to combine the cobbler mixture. After the meat and vegetables are cooked, gently roll out the cobbler mix and cut it into rounds.

9. Place the rounds on top of the cooked meat and bake for 15–20 minutes at 200°C/gas mark 6, or until the cobbler is well risen and golden on top.

SERVES 5–6

Oriental Beef Pancakes

This dish is similar to an Italian cannelloni because it uses filled pancakes in a sauce. It is an unusual and tasty way to cook minced beef. Most supermarkets sell the oriental pancakes and hoisin sauce used in this recipe. Four pancakes per person is a reasonable portion as they are only small, but it is up to you how many you use. Any meat left over from the filling is added to the sauce. Don't be tempted to add any extra salt, though, as the soy and hoisin are very salty indeed.

For the pancakes

1 small onion, chopped finely
A tablespoon sunflower oil
A teaspoon sesame oil – optional, but it adds flavour
3 garlic cloves, chopped finely
700g minced beef, or an equal mixture of beef and pork mince
2 tablespoons hoisin sauce, mixed into 4 tablespoons water
1 tablespoon soy sauce
16 oriental pancakes

For the sauce

1 red pepper, chopped
Sunflower oil, for frying
6 medium open-cup mushrooms, sliced
2 garlic cloves, chopped
2 tablespoons tomato purée
125ml dry white wine
2 tablespoons hoisin sauce, mixed with 4 tablespoons water
A dash of soy sauce

To make the pancakes

1. Fry the onion in the oil. Add the sesame oil also if you are using it.

2. Add the garlic and minced meat and fry until the meat is brown.

3. Stir in the sauces and cook gently for 15 minutes.

4. Place a tablespoon of the meat mixture into the centre of each pancake and roll up. Place in an ovenproof dish, packed tightly together.

To make the sauce

1. Fry the pepper in a little oil and add the mushrooms, garlic and tomato purée. When the juices start to run from the mushrooms, add the wine.

2. Stir in any leftover meat from the filling and add the other sauces.

3. Cook for 5 minutes, then pour over the pancakes.

4. Place in the oven for about 20 minutes at 150°C/gas mark 2 to heat through.

Serving suggestion
Serve with either egg-fried rice or noodles dressed with a little soy sauce.

SERVES 5–6

Surprise Burgers

These can be made with lamb or beef mince. As for the cheese filling, any cheese will do, but I find that Cheddar, feta and haloumi stand up most successfully to the rigours of being fried.

- 500g minced beef or lamb
- 1 clove of garlic, chopped or grated
- ½ teaspoon chopped fresh rosemary or ¼ teaspoon of dried
- 1 tablespoon tomato purée
- ½ teaspoon ground cumin
- ½ teaspoon paprika
- Salt and pepper to taste
- About 100g of cheese, cubed

1. In a bowl, mix the meat and all the other ingredients together except for the cheese. I find it best to use my hands and massage the seasonings into the meat.

2. Divide the mixture into 8–10 balls and squash down with a spatula, or use a food ring to form the burgers.

3. Press your finger into the centre of each burger and drop in 1 or 2 cubes of cheese. Squeeze the meat up over the cheese to cover.

4. Fry each burger, 3–4 at a time, in a frying pan, or place them on an oiled baking sheet and put in the oven for 15–20 minutes at 190°C/gas mark 5 until cooked. Serve with bread buns and salad.

Variations

• Omit the paprika, rosemary and cumin and instead use ½ teaspoon of chilli flakes and 1 tablespoon sweet chilli sauce.

• If using lamb, add a dessertspoon of freshly chopped mint to the meat as well as the other ingredients in the original recipe.

SERVES 6

Roast Belly Pork with Lemon and Parsley Stuffing

This recipe requires white breadcrumbs. These can be made in a food processor or grated using the fine side of your grater.

80g white breadcrumbs
Juice of 2 small or 1½ large lemons and grated zest from half
Half a small onion, chopped finely or grated
2 tablespoons fresh parsley, chopped
Salt and pepper to taste
1.5–2kg boned belly pork

1. Make the stuffing by soaking the breadcrumbs in the lemon juice and mixing in the zest, onion, parsley and seasoning.

2. Flatten the pork with the meat side uppermost and spread the stuffing over evenly.

3. Roll up the meat and secure the roll with string.

4. Dry the skin of the joint and rub in a little salt.

5. Roast skin-side up at 220°C/gas mark 7 for 20 minutes, then turn down the heat to 180°C/gas mark 4 and cook for 1½ hours. The meat should be tender and the skin crispy.

Spicy Pork and Tomato Casserole

SERVES 5–6

You can use the cheapest cut of pork meat and cut into bite-sized pieces.

Oil for frying
1 onion, chopped
1 red pepper, chopped
1 courgette, sliced thinly
2 garlic cloves, chopped
1 heaped tablespoon plain flour
1 teaspoon paprika
1 teaspoon mild chilli powder
500g diced pork meat
400g canned chopped tomatoes
2 teaspoons soy sauce
Juice of half a lemon

1. Heat the oil in a frying pan and fry the onion until translucent. Add the pepper and the courgette and fry for 2–3 minutes; stir in the garlic. Transfer to an ovenproof dish.

2. Sieve the flour, paprika and chilli powder into a bowl. Roll the meat in the seasoned flour and coat well.

3. Using the same pan the vegetables were in, fry the pork gently until it changes colour. Add to the onion and vegetables. Add 2–3 tablespoons of water to the frying pan to remove the juices, then pour this over the meat.

4. Add the tomatoes and stir in the soy sauce and lemon juice. Season to taste, but remembering that soy sauce is very salty.

5. Cover and cook in the oven for 45 minutes at 190°C /gas mark 5, then raise the heat to 200°C/gas mark 6 and cook for 15 minutes. Serve with boiled rice or potato wedges and a green vegetable.

SERVES 5–6

Pork in Red Wine

You can use shoulder or leg of pork steak in this recipe. Shoulder is cheaper and needs a slightly longer cooking time, so if you do use it, cut it into smaller pieces and cook for longer.

Oil for frying
1 onion, chopped
800g pork steak
½ teaspoon paprika
3 garlic cloves, chopped
1 tablespoon balsamic vinegar
1 tablespoon tomato purée
Pinch of dried sage
Salt and pepper to taste
Half a bottle of red wine
A little double cream
2 tablespoons chopped fresh parsley

1. Heat the oil in a saucepan and fry the onion until soft.

2. Add the pork, sprinkle in the paprika and stir in the garlic and balsamic vinegar. Cook for a few minutes, until the pork is lightly cooked all over.

3. Stir in the tomato purée and sage. Season to taste.

4. Pour in the wine and bring to the boil. As soon as it is boiling, transfer it to an ovenproof casserole dish.

5. Cover and cook at 180°C/gas mark 4 for 1¼ hours if using leg of pork, 1½ hours if using shoulder.

6. Ten minutes before the end of cooking, stir in a little double cream and the fresh parsley. Serve with gnocchi (Italian potato dumplings) or some fresh pasta.

Spanish-style Pork Meatballs

SERVES 5–6

For the meatballs
500g minced pork
2 garlic cloves, crushed
2 tablespoons tomato purée
Oil for frying

For the sauce
1 tablespoon olive oil
1 onion, chopped finely
1 red pepper, chopped
A small glass red wine
500ml passata
50g pitted black olives

To make the meatballs

1. Mix the first 3 ingredients together in a bowl. Form into 16 balls (allow 4 per person).

2. Fry the meatballs gently in a little hot oil, then transfer to an ovenproof dish.

To make the sauce

1. Heat the olive oil in a frying pan and fry the onion and pepper. Add the wine and passata. Cook for 5 minutes, then stir in the black olives.

2. Pour the sauce over the meatballs. Cover and cook in a preheated oven for 30 minutes at 180°C/gas mark 4.

SERVES 4

Cheesy Toad-in-the-hole

This is a tasty twist on the traditional sausages baked in a Yorkshire pudding. It can also be an easy labour-saving meal – if you make your batter the day before.

180g plain flour
2 eggs
600ml milk
8 thick pork sausages
Lard for greasing
100g Cheddar, grated
Salt and pepper to taste

1. Preheat the oven to 220°C/gas mark 7.

2. Sift the flour into a mixing bowl. Blend in the eggs with a wooden spoon.

3. Whisk in the milk gradually and continue to whisk until small bubbles appear on the surface of the mixture. Leave to stand while the sausages are prepared.

4. In a frying pan over a medium heat, lightly brown the sausages all over. Either leave them whole or cut each one in half and brown the centre.

5. Grease a baking tin or ovenproof dish with lard – this heats to a higher temperature than oil – and arrange the sausages over the bottom of the tin.

6. Stir half of the cheese into the prepared batter and pour it around the sausages.

7. Sprinkle the rest of the cheese over the sausage and the batter.

8. Bake immediately in the preheated oven for 25–30 minutes, or until the pudding has risen around the sausage and is brown and crisp.

SERVES 4

J and A's Chickpea and Chorizo Stew

750g new potatoes, scrubbed and skins left on
Oil for frying
1 medium onion, chopped
1 red pepper, chopped
2 garlic cloves, chopped
1 tablespoon honey
1 level teaspoon paprika
80–100g chorizo sausage, chopped
400g canned chopped tomatoes
450g canned chickpeas

1. Put the potatoes in a saucepan with enough hot, salted water to cover and bring to the boil.

2. Meanwhile, heat the oil in a frying pan and fry the onion and pepper until soft.

3. Stir in the garlic, honey, paprika and chorizo. Leave on a very low heat for 5 minutes to allow the flavours to develop.

4. Drain the potatoes when tender. Put back in the pan and add the canned tomatoes.

5. Stir in the chorizo mixture and add the chickpeas. Cook on a low heat for 5 minutes.

Serving suggestion
Serve with some good crusty bread dressed with a little olive oil and balsamic vinegar.

SERVES 4–5

Leek and Ham Layer

Bacon and ham are wonderful ingredients. They make tasty dishes reasonably economically, because you need much smaller amounts than other meats, due to their rich flavour.

300ml milk
1 level tablespoon cornflour, mixed with 2 tablespoons milk
½ teaspoon mustard or mustard powder
Salt and pepper to taste
3 large potatoes, peeled and sliced into .5cm slices
A knob of butter
2 large leeks, sliced thinly
300g diced cooked ham or bacon
Grated cheese for the topping

1. Preheat the oven to 200°C/gas mark 6.

2. Make a white sauce by heating the milk in a microwave or saucepan until hot (but not boiling) and pouring it over the cornflour mixture. Stir in the mustard and seasoning and return to the pan. Bring to the boil, stirring all the time with a wooden spoon, then turn down the heat and simmer for 2 minutes.

3. Boil the potatoes for 4 minutes. Drain.

4. Heat the butter in a saucepan and sauté the leeks until tender. Spoon half of them into a buttered ovenproof dish, then scatter half of the ham over the leeks and add a potato layer on top. Repeat this, finishing with a thick layer of potato.

5. Pour over the white sauce and top with the grated cheese.

6. Cook in the oven for 20–25 minutes at 200°C/gas mark 6, or until the top begins to brown. Serve with broad or French green beans.

Broccoli and Bacon Bake

SERVES 2–3

This recipe uses the same quantity of white sauce made in the previous recipe. Just follow the directions for it and add 50–60g of mature or smoked Cheddar to the sauce before pouring over the dish.

200g steamed broccoli
6 bacon rashers, grilled until just crisp
Salt and pepper to taste
300ml white sauce (see above)
50–60g Cheddar, either mature or smoked

1. Place the cooked broccoli in a buttered ovenproof dish and cut each cooked bacon rasher into 3 pieces. Arrange around the broccoli. Season to taste.

2. Pour over the cheese sauce and bake for 10 minutes in a hot oven, or place under the grill until the top browns. For crispiness, sprinkle 2 tablespoons of breadcrumbs over the top before browning. Serve with crusty bread.

SERVES 4

Cheesy Bacon Bake

Another quick, easy and tasty recipe using bacon.

1 large onion, chopped
4–5 medium potatoes, peeled and cut into chunks
Salt and pepper to taste
100–150g Cheddar, grated
8 rashers of bacon

1. Preheat the oven to 200°C/gas mark 6.

2. Boil the onions and potatoes together in a pan with sufficient salted water just to cover them. Cook until just tender.

3. Drain the potatoes and onions and put them into a buttered ovenproof dish.

4. Season to taste and sprinkle the potatoes with the grated cheese; use as much as you like.

5. Place the rashers of bacon over the potato mixture.

6. Put in the oven and bake until the bacon is fully cooked – about 20 minutes.

Serving suggestion
Serve with fresh green peas or any green vegetable. Sweetcorn is also an excellent accompaniment.

SERVES 4

Joshua's Sausage Casserole

Our son Joshua had this idea for a very tasty recipe and cooked it for us one evening. It is now one of our favourites.

- Oil for frying
- 1 medium onion, chopped
- 1 red pepper, chopped
- 8 open-cup mushrooms, halved
- 2 garlic cloves, chopped
- 2 tablespoons tomato purée
- 8 good pork sausages
- 1 level teaspoon paprika
- 1 tablespoon honey
- 100g chorizo sausages, cut into cubes – or sliced and quartered
- 400g canned tomatoes
- ½ teaspoon of dried rosemary
- 1 tablespoon sweet chilli sauce
- 3–4 tablespoons Parmesan

1. Preheat the oven to 190°C/gas mark 5.

2. Heat the oil in a frying pan and fry the onion and pepper for 2–3 minutes, until softened, then add the mushrooms and garlic.

3. Stir in the tomato purée and place in an ovenproof casserole dish.

4. Slice the pork sausages into bite-sized pieces and fry gently in the pan.

5. Drain off any excess fat and sprinkle the paprika over the sausages. Drizzle with honey while continuing to cook gently.

6. Add the chorizo sausages, stir, then add the contents of the pan to the casserole with the onions.

7. Pour the tomatoes over the sausages and stir in the rosemary and sweet chilli sauce.

8. Sprinkle the cheese over the sausage mixture, cover and cook for 30–40 minutes.

Serving suggestion
Serve with baked potatoes and a green vegetable. Sprouts and steamed spring greens go really well.

SERVES 5–6

Braised Shoulder of Lamb

Use a lidded dish or pan that you can cook with both on the hob and in the oven.

- 1–1.5kg shoulder of lamb
- 4 rashers streaky bacon, chopped into 1cm pieces
- 1 large onion, chopped
- 2 medium carrots, sliced
- Approximately 100g diced swede
- 2 celery sticks, diced
- ½ teaspoon each of thyme and rosemary
- Salt and black pepper to taste
- 280ml lamb stock or water

1. Trim any fat from the lamb and put it into a frying pan along with the bacon. Cook gently for 2–3 minutes without crisping the bacon.

2. Add the onion and cook for 2 minutes, then add the rest of the vegetables and cook for 3–4 minutes.

3. Transfer the lot to the dish or pan you are using for the rest of the cooking and add the herbs and seasoning.

4. Pour the stock or water over the meat and cover. Simmer gently for 1 hour.

5. Take off the lid and place in a preheated oven at 200°C/gas mark 6 for another 45 minutes, or until the meat is brown on the top.

6. Transfer the meat and vegetables to a warmed serving dish and pour the stock into a pan. Keep the meat and vegetables warm while reducing the stock, then pour over the meat to serve.

SERVES 5–6

Lamb Tagine

This is based on the North African dish. It is cooked slowly for a long period of time, which means the lamb almost melts in your mouth. Some recipes also contain dates and other dried fruits; add some if you prefer, but I find it too sweet. You don't need a tagine to cook this recipe – an ordinary casserole dish will do.

- 1 tablespoon sunflower or vegetable oil
- 2 teaspoons paprika
- ½ teaspoon cayenne
- 1 teaspoon each of turmeric, ground cumin and coriander
- ½ teaspoon cinnamon
- 1 teaspoon dried mint
- 500g lamb neck meat, cut into 2cm pieces
- 1 large onion, sliced finely
- 2 garlic cloves, chopped
- 2 tablespoons honey
- 350ml lamb or vegetable stock (see page 19)
- 400g canned tomatoes
- 8 dried apricots, halved
- 50g flaked almonds
- Salt and pepper to taste
- 2 tablespoons chopped fresh parsley

1. Preheat the oven to 150°C/gas mark 2.

2. Combine the oil, spices and dried herbs in a large bowl. Add the meat and coat in the spicy mixture. Cover and leave overnight.

3. Fry the onion in a little oil until just soft. Transfer to a casserole dish – or a tagine, if you have one.

4. Fry the meat gently until lightly brown all over. Add the garlic and drizzle over the honey. Transfer to the casserole dish with the onions. Deglaze the pan by adding a little hot water and mixing it with the juices; this makes sure you don't lose any of the flavours. Pour over the meat and onions.

5. Stir the stock into the meat and add the tomatoes, apricots and almonds. Season and stir to combine.

6. Cover and cook for 2–2½ hours, or until the meat is melting into the juices.

7. Sprinkle the parsley over the tagine just before serving.

Serving suggestion
Serve with couscous or boiled rice and a green salad.

SERVES 4

Moussaka

For the meat sauce
900g aubergines, thinly sliced lengthways
Salt and black pepper to taste
Oil for frying
1 large onion, chopped
400–450g minced lamb
2 garlic cloves, chopped
1 tablespoon plain flour
220g canned chopped tomatoes
125ml dry white wine
½ teaspoon each dried oregano and basil
3 tablespoons tomato purée
Butter for greasing
100g fresh breadcrumbs

For the white sauce
15g butter
1 tablespoon flour
300ml milk
100g Cheddar, plus extra for topping
1 egg yolk

1. Sprinkle the strips of aubergines with salt and leave in a colander to allow some of the liquid to drain away. This will take about 30 minutes.

2. Heat the oil in a frying pan and fry the onions until soft. Add the lamb and garlic and cook until the lamb is lightly brown.

3. Sprinkle over the flour and stir in the tomatoes, wine, herbs and tomato purée. Season to taste and simmer gently for 25–30 minutes.

4. Rinse and pat the aubergines dry with kitchen paper or a clean tea cloth. Heat a little oil in another frying pan and fry them quickly, a few at a time, until slightly brown on one side.

5. Butter an ovenproof dish, then layer it first with the meat, then the aubergines, and repeat finishing with a layer of meat.

6. Preheat the oven to 180°C/gas mark 4.

7. To make the white sauce, melt the butter in a saucepan over a gentle heat and stir in the flour. Remove from the heat and gradually whisk or beat in the milk. Return to the heat and bring to the boil, stirring continuously. Cook over a low heat for 2 minutes. Stir in the cheese and egg yolk and pour over the meat and aubergines.

8. Top with the breadcrumbs and a little extra cheese if you wish.

9. Bake in the oven for 50–60 minutes, or until the top begins to brown. If you like a crispy top, put the dish under the grill for a few minutes before serving. Leave it to settle for 5 minutes before serving.

Serving suggestion
Serve with a green salad and crusty bread.

Sticky Chicken

SERVES 4–6

4 chicken thighs and 4 chicken drumsticks
3 tablespoons honey
1 tablespoon soy sauce
2 tablespoons sweet chilli sauce
3 garlic cloves, grated
1 tablespoon balsamic vinegar

1. Preheat the oven to 190°C/gas mark 5.

2. Place the chicken pieces on a baking tray.

3. In a bowl, mix all the other ingredients together and pour evenly over the chicken. Any sauce that rolls off the meat can be mopped up with the underside of the chicken portions.

4. Roast in the preheated oven for about 35–40 minutes.

One-pan Chicken

SERVES 4

This really is cooked all in one pan. As long as it is a large frying pan, all the ingredients will fit in. Cutting the chicken, onion and pepper into small pieces means they cook much quicker.

A little olive oil for frying
1 onion, chopped into small pieces
4 rashers bacon
1 red pepper, chopped into small pieces
2 garlic cloves, grated
40–50g chopped chorizo sausage
450g chicken thigh meat, cut into small pieces
450g small new potatoes, boiled with the skins on and cut in half
Salt and pepper to taste

1. Heat the olive oil in a frying pan and fry the onion, bacon and pepper together. When the onion is soft, add the garlic and chorizo. Keep over a medium heat so that nothing burns.

2. Add the chicken and stir into the other ingredients. When the chicken has fried for a few minutes, cover the pan. If you haven't a lid for your frying pan, just use some aluminium foil.

3. Cook over a low heat until the chicken is cooked through, then add the cooked potatoes. Squash them among all the other ingredients and cover the frying pan again until the potatoes are hot and have taken up some of the juices.

4. Serve straight from the pan with corn on the cob.

SERVES 4

Chicken in White Wine

This is similar to a tapas dish we once tried in a restaurant. It was so good, but I've had to guess the ingredients for this version because they wouldn't tell me!

- 4 garlic cloves, chopped
- 8 chicken thighs, skinned and boned
- 200ml dry white wine
- 8 ground black peppercorns
- A little olive oil for frying
- Salt to taste
- 1 tablespoon chopped fresh chives
- 1 tub crème fraîche
- 2 tablespoons chopped fresh parsley

1. Rub the garlic into the chicken and place in a dish. Pour over the white wine and ground peppercorns. Leave to marinate for 1½ hours.

2. Lift the chicken out of the marinade and fry in a large frying pan with a little olive oil. When the chicken begins to brown, pour in the marinade and bring to the boil. Reduce the sauce slightly and season with salt to taste.

3. Add the chives and turn the heat down to simmering. When the chicken is cooked, stir in the crème fraîche and parsley and turn off the heat.

Serving suggestion
Serve with boiled rice and salad.

SERVES 4–6

Chicken Curry

- 1kg chicken portions, thighs and drumsticks or a whole chicken jointed into 6 pieces
- 30g butter or ghee
- 2 large onions, sliced
- 250ml plain yoghurt
- 4 tablespoons milk
- 50g sultanas
- 25g flaked almonds

For the spice mix

- 1 teaspoon each of ground coriander, cumin, turmeric and poppy seeds
- ½ teaspoon of chilli powder
- 2cm piece of fresh ginger, grated
- ½ level teaspoon cinnamon
- 2 cloves
- 3 cardamom pods: open by cutting off the end to release the seeds
- 4 black peppercorns
- 1 garlic clove, grated finely
- 1 level teaspoon salt

1. First make the spice mix. In a mortar, mix all the spices, garlic and salt together, grinding them into each other with a pestle. Add 2 tablespoons of water and mix into a thick paste.

2. Loosen the skin of the chicken pieces and rub the spice mixture into the meat. Leave to rest for 30 minutes.

3. Meanwhile, heat half the butter in a large frying pan and fry the onions very gently for about 10–12 minutes, or until lightly browned.

4. Remove the onions with a slotted spoon, leaving as much of the butter behind as you can; reserve them in a dish. Use the pan to brown the chicken pieces all over. Transfer the chicken to a large, lidded casserole and pour over any juices.

5. Preheat the oven to 190°C/gas mark 5.

6. Put the yogurt and milk in a saucepan and heat gently to simmering. Stir the cooked onions into the yoghurt mixture and pour over the chicken.

7. Cover the dish and place in the oven for 1–1½ hours. Check halfway through the cooking time that the sauce isn't bubbling too much; if it is, turn the heat down to 180°C/gas mark 4.

8. To finish the dish, heat the rest of the butter or ghee in a small frying pan and cook the sultanas for a few minutes. Sprinkle them and the almonds over the cooked chicken and serve with boiled rice.

SERVES 4

Turkey and Pepper Kebabs with Redcurrant Chutney

These are great cooked on the barbecue, grilled or roasted in the oven. Use a red, green and yellow pepper for a colourful dish. Serve with the delicious sweet chutney.

500g turkey meat, breast or leg, cut into 2cm chunks
2 tablespoons honey
1 tablespoon balsamic vinegar
Juice of 1 lime
3 peppers, cut into 2–3cm squares
8 large closed-cup mushrooms, cut in half
2 medium onions, cut into thick slices
Salt to taste

For the chutney
Olive oil for frying
1 small onion, finely chopped
180g redcurrants
2 Granny Smith apples, peeled and diced
110g soft brown sugar
150ml balsamic vinegar
¼ teaspoon each of cinnamon and chilli powder
½ teaspoon salt

1. To make the chutney, heat a little olive oil in a frying pan or large saucepan and fry the onions until they are soft, then add all the other ingredients.

2. Cook over a low heat until all the sugar has dissolved. Turn up the heat and bring to the boil. Turn down the heat and simmer for 20–25 minutes, or until the chutney is thick and glossy. Allow to cool for 20 minutes before pouring into a sterilised jar with a close-fitting lid. This will keep for 2 weeks in the fridge.

3. Put the turkey in a bowl and pour over the honey, balsamic vinegar and and lime juice. Stir well and leave to marinate for 2 hours.

4. Thread the meat, peppers, mushrooms and onions alternately onto bamboo or metal skewers. Leave a few centimetres at each end for ease of holding. Season to taste.

5. Put onto a lightly oiled baking tray and drizzle with the rest of the marinade.

6. Cook on a barbecue or under a hot grill, turning now and again until cooked through, or put into a hot oven for 20–30 minutes. Serve the cooked kebabs with the chutney and some salad leaves.

SERVES 4–6

Turkey Chilli

You can use fresh chillies in this recipe if you wish. Personally, I would exchange the chilli flakes for a small green and red chilli, chopped finely.

1 tablespoon oil
1 large onion, chopped
1 celery stick, chopped
1 courgette, diced
2 tablespoons tomato purée
500g minced turkey
1 teaspoon chilli flakes
120ml red wine
2 garlic cloves, chopped
400g canned tomatoes or 500ml passata
50g red lentils
Salt to taste
400g canned red kidney beans

1. Heat the oil in a frying pan and fry the onion for 2–3 minutes, then add the celery and courgette.

2. Stir in the tomato purée and add the meat. Cook gently until the turkey has changed colour. If your pan isn't large enough to continue cooking the chilli, then transfer the mixture to a large saucepan.

3. Add the chilli flakes, red wine and garlic, then stir in the tomatoes or passata. Bring to the boil, then turn down the heat to simmering and stir in the red lentils. Season with salt to taste.

4. Cover and simmer gently for 45 minutes. Stir in the drained kidney beans and cook for 10 more minutes.

5. Leave to settle for a few minutes before serving.

Serving suggestion
If you can, allow the chilli to cool for 2 hours before reheating to piping hot and serving with boiled rice, baked potatoes or crusty bread. This allows all the flavours to develop and makes it taste much better.

FISH DISHES

At present, fish can be very expensive to serve to your family, but there are some great-tasting varieties that (literally) don't cost the earth. For white-fish dishes, whiting, coley and pollack are really good alternatives to cod and haddock, stocks of which are currently declining. When choosing oily fish, mackerel, herring and sardines are reasonably priced and make satisfying meals.

Grilled Mackerel with Lemon and Herb Crust

SERVES 4

- 1 tablespoon fresh parsley, chopped
- 1 tablespoon freshly chopped dill
- 1 teaspoon thyme leaves
- 50g fresh breadcrumbs
- Freshly ground black pepper to taste
- 4 tablespoons lemon juice
- Salt to taste
- 4 mackerel, gutted, washed and heads cut off if you wish
- 2 tablespoons olive oil

1. Combine the herbs, breadcrumbs, pepper and lemon juice and salt to taste.

2. Make some slits in both sides of the fish and push a little of the herb mixture into each slit.

3. Drizzle the fish with the olive oil and coat with the rest of the herb mixture.

4. Place on a baking sheet and grill for 6–7 minutes each side. Baste the fish occasionally with any juices that begin to run.

Serving suggestion

Serve with some boiled new potatoes topped with a little extra fresh parsley and a knob of butter.

Oat-coated Herrings with Crispy Bacon

SERVES 4

Use ordinary porridge oats for this recipe.

Salt and pepper to taste
4 herrings, filleted
100g oatmeal
A little oil for frying
3–4 rashers of bacon, chopped into small pieces
Lemon wedges
Sprigs of fresh parsley

1. Season the fish fillets and roll them in the oatmeal.

2. Heat the oil in a frying pan and fry the bacon until it is just cooked.

3. Add the fish and fry with the bacon for 3–4 minutes each side. The bacon will crisp up by the time the fish are cooked.

4. Serve with the lemon wedges and parsley.

Sardines with Tapenade and Roasted Cherry Tomatoes

SERVES 4

20 cherry tomatoes
A little olive oil
Salt to taste
3–4 sardines per person, washed and gutted

For the tapenade
25 black or black and green olives
3 garlic cloves, crushed
4 anchovy fillets in olive oil

1. Preheat the oven to 200°C/gas mark 6.

2. Put the tomatoes into a roasting pan, drizzle with a little olive oil and sprinkle with some salt. Place in the oven and roast for 20 minutes, or until they just begin to burst and brown.

3. Meanwhile, mash all the tapenade ingredients together in a mortar.

4. Place the fish on an oiled baking sheet and push a little tapenade into the belly opening of each fillet. Spread the rest over the sardines.

5. Put in the oven and cook for 10–15 minutes along with the tomatoes.

Serving suggestion
Serve as a starter or with a salad and crusty bread as a main course.

SERVES 4

Fish and Potato Layer

3 medium potatoes, peeled and cut into 5mm slices
700g white fish fillets: coley, pollack or whiting
350ml milk
40g butter, plus extra for greasing
2 tablespoons plain flour
½ level teaspoon mustard powder
100g mature Cheddar
Salt and pepper to taste

1. In a saucepan, boil the potato slices in just enough water to cover them until just cooked but not falling apart. This should take about 6 minutes, depending on the variety of potatoes.

2. Poach the fish in the milk for 5 minutes. Lift out the fish and reserve the milk in a jug.

3. Butter an ovenproof dish and put in a layer of fish, then potato. Repeat and finish with a potato layer.

4. Make a white sauce by melting the butter in a saucepan over a low heat. Stir in the flour and mustard. Remove from the heat and gradually stir in the poaching milk.

5. Return to the heat and bring to the boil. If it thickens too much, add a little more milk.

6. Stir in the cheese and season with salt and black pepper to taste.

7. Pour the sauce over the fish and potatoes evenly, tapping the dish to allow the sauce to reach the lower layers. Sprinkle with a little more cheese if you wish.

8. Place under a hot grill until the top browns. Serve with peas or broccoli.

Variation
For a crispy top, use 50g fresh breadcrumbs mixed with a little grated cheese and spread on the top of your fish dish before grilling.

SERVES 4

Battered Whiting

This is the lightest batter I have ever eaten, and its consistency is helped by the addition of baking powder. Make sure your oil is very hot before cooking the fish as the batter will cook straight away and form a barrier against the oil. In this way the fish will steam inside the batter and keep all its delicious flavour locked in.

Oil for frying
4 pieces of fish, each weighing about 200–250g

For the batter
200g self-raising flour
½ teaspoon baking powder
1 teaspoon salt
300ml water

1. First make the batter by sieving the flour, baking powder and salt together into a bowl.

2. Whisk in the water gradually to make a batter with a smooth, creamy consistency.

3. Heat the oil in a deep-fat fryer or deep-sided pan. Test the temperature by dropping in a small cube of bread; if it browns within a minute, the oil is ready.

4. Pat each fish fillet dry with a kitchen towel, then dip it in the batter. Wipe off any excess on the side of the bowl and place each fillet carefully in the pan. (I'm a coward, so I use tongs for this step!)

5. The fish should take about 7-8 minutes to cook. Turn the fillets over in the oil if necessary. Serve with crispy chips and chip-shop-style mushy peas.

COOKING WITH CHEAPER CUTS

My Notes

5
Pasta and Rice

Where would we be without these ingredients? You just wouldn't believe the difference between homemade pasta and fresh pasta bought from the shops. In our house, making pasta is always the cue for floured clothes and handprints in unmentionable places (especially if my husband, Paul, helps me!), but I think you, too, will succumb to the temptation of making a mess – it's just so much fun. And of course, making your own pasta is inexpensive and always gives a better flavour.

Rice is not a beginner's experience. It can be hard to get it just right, and no two cooks do it in the same way, but perseverance at getting it how you want it is always rewarded by empty plates and smiling faces.

PASTA DISHES

Homemade Pasta

This is sufficient to feed four hungry people, but don't be afraid to make double and freeze some: it is good to freeze for up to 2 months. The successful ratio is 110g flour to 1 egg, so make as much as you wish.

You don't need a pasta maker, but it does make life a lot easier when you require thin sheets or tagliatelle-type pasta. You can roll out your pasta with a rolling pin and cut it to the size and shape required.

I find it easier to make on my work surface than in a bowl, but try both and see which is easier for you.

330g plain white flour, plus extra for rolling out
½ level teaspoon salt
3 eggs
Spoonful of cornmeal or polenta, for rolling out

1. Sieve the flour and salt together, either into a bowl or directly onto the work surface.

2. Make a well in the centre and break in the eggs.

3. Mix with your fingertips, making sure all the egg is incorporated into the flour.

4. When all is combined, knead the dough for about 10 minutes, or until it is smooth and pliable.

5. Leave it covered in cling film for 30–40 minutes before using. Make sure it is well covered or it will dry out.

6. It is now ready to be rolled out, shaped or put through a pasta maker. Use a little flour mixed with a spoonful of cornmeal or polenta for the rolling-out process; it will keep the pasta from sticking together.

7. To cook fresh pasta, have a large pan of salted boiling water ready and drop in the pasta. Cook for 2–3 minutes, depending on how thick the pasta is. Drain well before serving.

Wholewheat Pasta

This requires more egg to flour than the homemade pasta recipe on the previous page. It also needs a little oil, because wholewheat flour soaks up the moisture.

180g plain white flour
200g wholewheat flour
½ teaspoon salt
4 eggs
1 dessertspoon olive oil

1. Prepare and cook the pasta in exactly the same way as in the homemade pasta recipe on the previous page, adding the oil along with the eggs.

2. Now make a delicious sauce, such as the pesto below, to cover it!

Homemade Pesto

This is the quickest pasta sauce to make and is a really tasty, traditional Italian sauce. It is best made in a food processor, but if you don't have one, use a large pestle and mortar.

30g pine nuts
40g basil leaves
2 garlic cloves
60g Parmesan
½ level teaspoon salt
125ml extra-virgin olive oil

1. Put all the ingredients into a food processor and whiz until it reaches your ideal texture. Alternatively, pound everything together in a mortar.

2. Serve with hot pasta and extra Parmesan if you wish.

Variation
You can vary this by adding 100g of sun-dried tomatoes instead of the basil and use the oil out of the tomatoes in place of the extra-virgin olive oil. Add a teaspoon of honey to balance out the flavour of the tomatoes.

SERVES 4–5

Bacon and Cheese Pasta Bake

I first made this when we didn't have enough bacon in the house to feed the five of us but I still needed to make a hearty meal. So it was going to be bacon-and-cheese macaroni-type dish. It has now developed into the following recipe. I have made this with most pasta shapes, and even spaghetti works well.

- 3–4 rashers bacon, chopped into small strips
- 2 garlic cloves, chopped
- 500ml milk
- 1 tablespoon cornflour
- 2 tablespoons chopped fresh chives
- ⅓ pack light soft cream cheese
- Black pepper to taste
- 150g mature Cheddar, grated
- 500g wholewheat pasta or 350g of homemade, any shape you like
- 50g breadcrumbs

1. Preheat the oven to 200°C/gas mark 6.

2. Fry the bacon gently in its own fat as much as possible, or add a little sunflower oil. Stir in the garlic and cook for 2 minutes.

3. Pour in all the milk except 2 tablespoons – use this to mix with the cornflour – and heat to simmer. Add the cornflour and milk paste and bring to the boil, stirring constantly.

4. Add the chives. Reduce the heat to a simmer for a few minutes to cook the cornflour, then add the cream cheese and stir it in well. Season with black pepper to taste.

5. Stir in half the Cheddar. Remove the sauce from the heat while you cook the pasta either according to the packet directions, or following the cooking instructions on page 74.

6. Put the pasta into an ovenproof dish and pour over the sauce.

7. Combine the rest of the cheese and the breadcrumbs and sprinkle over the top. Bake for 8–10 minutes, or until the top is golden brown, and serve with a crunchy salad.

Variation
If you wish, you can serve the sauce and pasta without putting it in the oven. Just sprinkle the top with the cheese and omit the breadcrumbs.

SERVES 4–5

Chicken Pasta Sauce

- 1 tablespoon olive oil for frying
- 2 small chicken breasts, chopped finely
- 2–3 garlic cloves, chopped
- 1 tablespoon tomato purée
- 500ml passata
- Salt and black pepper to taste
- Fresh or dried pasta of your choice: allow 125–150g per person of fresh, or 100–120g per person of dried
- 250ml crème fraîche
- Grated Parmesan or Grana Padano for serving

1. Heat the olive oil in a large frying pan and fry the chicken and garlic together gently until cooked. Stir in the tomato purée.

2. Pour in the passata and simmer for 10 minutes. Add a little salt and black pepper to taste.

3. Cook the pasta either according to the packet directions, or following the cooking instructions on page 74 if using homemade.

4. Stir in the crème fraîche, spoon the sauce over the pasta and serve with Parmesan or Grana Padano cheese.

SERVES 4

Seafood in White Wine Pasta Sauce

This is a luxurious seafood-lover's pasta sauce – and one of my own favourites.

- 1 tablespoon olive oil for frying
- 2–3 shallots, chopped finely
- 2 garlic cloves, chopped
- 100g fresh mussels, shelled
- 100g prawns, shelled
- 125ml dry white wine
- Fresh or dried pasta of your choice: allow 125–150g per person of fresh, or 100–120g per person of dried
- Salt and black pepper to taste
- 250ml crème fraîche, or 125ml plus 4 tablespoons double cream
- 1 tablespoon chopped fresh parsley

1. Heat the oil in a large frying pan or saucepan and fry the shallots until soft. Add the garlic and seafood.

2. Add the wine and simmer for 2–3 minutes, stirring occasionally.

3. Cook the pasta either according to the packet directions, or following the cooking instructions on page 74 if using homemade.

4. Season to taste and add the crème fraîche and parsley. Remove from the heat while stirring the sauce.

5. Serve immediately with the cooked pasta.

SERVES 3–4

Roasted Tomato and Chilli Pasta Sauce

- 6 large or 8 medium tomatoes
- 1 red pepper
- Olive oil for roasting
- Salt to taste
- 2 garlic cloves
- 1 red chilli pepper, sliced finely or ½ teaspoon of chilli flakes
- 2 tablespoons sun-dried tomato purée
- 75ml dry white wine
- 1 dessertspoon balsamic vinegar
- Handful of basil leaves, optional

1. Preheat the oven to 220°C/gas mark 7.

2. Cut the tomatoes in half and the red pepper into strips. Place on a baking sheet and drizzle with olive oil and a little salt. Roast in the oven for 20–25 minutes, or until they are browning.

3. Put the cooked tomato and pepper in a pan and add the garlic and chilli and heat gently.

4. Stir in the tomato purée, wine and balsamic vinegar and simmer for 10 minutes, stirring occasionally.

5. Cook fresh or dried pasta of your choice (allow 125–150g per person of fresh, or 100–120g per person of dried) either according to the packet directions, or following the cooking instructions on page 74 if using homemade.

6. Serve the sauce with the pasta, and sprinkle with basil leaves, if using.

Quick Tuna Pasta Sauce

SERVES 3–4

- Olive oil for frying
- 1 small onion, chopped
- 1 garlic clove
- 3 tablespoons tomato purée mixed with 3 tablespoons water
- 3 anchovy fillets
- 185g canned tuna in oil, drained, but reserve 1 tablespoon of oil
- 200g canned chopped tomatoes
- Salt and black pepper to taste

1. Heat the oil in a frying pan and fry the onion until soft. Add the garlic and stir in the tomato purée and the anchovies.

2. Add the tuna, tuna oil and the tomatoes and simmer for 5 minutes. Season to taste.

3. Cook fresh or dried pasta of your choice (allow 125–150g per person of fresh, or 100–120g per person of dried) either according to the packet directions, or following the cooking instructions on page 74 if using homemade.

4. Serve the sauce with the pasta.

Serving suggestion

Try making your own thick ribbon pasta to use with this sauce.

Ravioli

To make homemade ravioli, I cut my rolled-out pasta with a biscuit cutter. Use any size you like and put a small amount of your filling of choice in the centre, then dampen the edges, fold and pinch the edges together. Allow to dry for about 15 minutes before cooking for 4 minutes in salted boiling water.

Below are 2 of my favourite ravioli fillings.

Bacon and Mushroom Ravioli

SERVES 4

- 4 rashers smoky bacon, chopped finely
- 6–8 chestnut mushrooms, chopped finely
- 2 garlic cloves, chopped
- Black pepper to taste
- 1 egg yolk
- 2 teaspoons single cream

1. In a small pan, cook the bacon and mushrooms together with the garlic.
2. Remove from the heat and cool for a few minutes. Season with black pepper and stir in the egg yolk and cream.
3. Fill the ravioli and cook for 4 minutes in boiling salted water.

Spinach, Ricotta and Parmesan

SERVES 4

- A knob of butter
- 200g fresh spinach, well washed
- Salt and pepper to taste
- A little grated nutmeg
- 50g ricotta cheese
- 50g Parmesan
- 1 egg yolk

1. Heat the butter in a saucepan over a medium heat and gently cook the spinach until completely wilted. Season with salt, pepper and a little nutmeg to taste.
2. Remove from the heat and mix in the ricotta, Parmesan and the egg yolk. Stir well.
3. Fill the ravioli and cook for 4 minutes in boiling salted water.

SERVES 4

Ragu Sauce

This sauce can be used to make a lasagne or fill cannelloni.

Olive oil for frying
2 medium onions, chopped
3 garlic cloves, chopped
4 rashers streaky bacon or pancetta, sliced into 1cm strips
350g minced pork
350g minced beef
4 tablespoons tomato purée
400g canned plum tomatoes
200ml red wine
A little grated nutmeg
Salt and pepper to taste
15g fresh basil leaves

1. In a large lidded pan, heat the olive oil and fry the onions until soft.

2. Add the garlic and bacon and cook for 2–3 minutes.

3. Add the pork and beef and cook until it the meat is brown and crumbly.

4. Add the tomato purée, tomatoes and red wine and stir in the nutmeg. Add any seasoning to taste.

5. Cover and cook for 1½ hours on a low simmer. Stir occasionally.

6. Add the basil and cook for 20 minutes more.

7. Cook fresh or dried pasta of your choice (allow 125–150g per person of fresh, or 100–120g per person of dried) either according to the packet directions, or following the cooking instructions on page 74 if using homemade. Serve the sauce with the pasta.

Variations
- Add 100g sliced mushrooms about an hour into the cooking time.
- Instead of basil, stir in some fresh thyme; a couple of sprigs will do.

Smoked Salmon Sauce

SERVES 4

100g pack smoked salmon
250ml light crème fraîche
A squeeze of lemon juice
50g prawns
Salt and black pepper to taste

1. Slice the salmon into thin strips and place in a pan. Heat gently, adding the crème fraîche and lemon juice.

2. Chop the prawns and add to the pan. Heat until it begins to bubble and season to taste.

3. Cook fresh or dried pasta of your choice (allow 125–150g per person of fresh, or 100–120g per person of dried) either according to the packet directions, or following the cooking instructions on page 74 if using homemade. Serve the sauce with the pasta immediately.

Serving suggestion
Tagliatelle goes very well with this sauce.

SERVES 4

Vegetable Pasta Sauce

A knob of butter
1 tablespoon olive oil
50g mushrooms, sliced
1 courgette, cut into baton-type strips
1 red onion, chopped finely
1 yellow and 1 red pepper, chopped
3 tablespoons sun-dried tomato purée
2 garlic cloves, chopped
125ml dry white wine
½ teaspoon dried thyme
½ teaspoon dried oregano
12 pitted black or green olives, halved or chopped if you prefer
Salt and pepper to taste
Fresh or dried pasta of your choice: allow 125–150g per person of fresh, or 100–120g per person of dried

1. Melt the butter in saucepan over a low heat. Add the oil, then sweat all the vegetables together, stirring for the first minute.

2. Cover and leave on a very low heat for 10 minutes. Stir in the tomato purée and garlic, cover again and leave for 5 more minutes.

3. Add the white wine and turn up the heat to a simmer.

4. Stir in the herbs and olives. Season to taste, then cover and cook gently for 10 minutes.

5. Cook the pasta of your choice either according to the packet directions, or following the cooking instructions on page 74 if using homemade.

6. Serve the sauce with the pasta.

SERVES 4

Chicken and Savoury Rice Casserole

Olive oil for frying
1 onion, chopped
1 red pepper, chopped
2 garlic cloves, chopped
50g frozen green beans, defrosted and chopped
50g chorizo sausage, diced into small pieces
4 chicken thighs
4 drumsticks
3 packs (3 x 120g) of savoury rice, either the chicken or golden variety
Sufficient boiling water to cover the rice

1. Preheat the oven to 190°C/gas mark 5.

2. Heat the oil in a frying pan and fry the onion, pepper and garlic until tender. Stir in the green beans, then put them into the bottom of an ovenproof dish or roasting pan. Add the chorizo sausage to the same dish and stir in evenly.

3. In the same pan, fry the chicken pieces – skin-side down for the thighs. Fry until brown, then turn over.

4. While the chicken is cooking, pour the rice over the vegetables and chorizo and stir. Pour water over the rice to cover well.

5. Arrange the chicken in the rice. Cover with foil and cook for 20 minutes in the preheated oven.

6. After 10 minutes, check to see whether the rice needs a little more boiling water and top up if necessary.

7. Make sure the chicken is well cooked before serving.

Serving suggestion
This goes really well served with sweetcorn.

SERVES 4

Quick Kedgeree

400g long-grain rice
80g frozen peas
1 tablespoon of sunflower oil
A knob of butter
1 dessertspoon turmeric
1 teaspoon ground cumin
½ teaspoon coriander
1 teaspoon garam masala
185g canned tuna, drained
3 hard-boiled eggs, shelled
1 tablespoon chopped fresh parsley

1. Cook the rice according to the packet instructions, adding the peas halfway through. Drain well.

2. In a large frying pan, add the oil and melt in the butter on a low heat.

3. Add the spices and stir in the rice. Cook for 2–3 minutes, stirring the spices into the rice.

4. Add the tuna and continue to stir.

5. Chop the eggs roughly and add to the rice mixture.

6. Serve immediately topped with fresh parsley.

Recipe tip
If the kedgeree looks too dry as it is cooking, add a tablespoon of water and an extra knob of butter.

Spanish Rice and Chicken

SERVES 3–4

This recipe uses up any leftover cooked chicken and tastes good, too.

A little oil for frying
1 medium onion, chopped
1 green pepper, chopped
400g long-grain rice
1 teaspoon chilli powder
½ teaspoon ground cumin
½ teaspoon ground black pepper
1 level teaspoon salt
1 tablespoon tomato purée
400ml chicken stock (see page 16)
400g canned tomatoes
250–300g cooked chicken, chopped

1. In a frying pan, heat the oil and fry the onion and pepper together until soft.

2. Add the rice, spices and tomato purée and fry very gently for 2 minutes.

3. Stir in the stock and canned tomatoes. Cook gently until the rice is tender. This will take about 20 minutes.

4. Add the chicken and heat through.

5. Serve immediately.

SERVES 3–4

Mushroom Risotto

Olive oil for frying
1 onion, finely chopped
800ml vegetable stock (see page 19)
4 large, flat mushrooms chopped as finely as you wish
6 closed-cup mushrooms, sliced
3 garlic cloves, chopped
350g arborio rice
120ml dry white wine
½ teaspoon thyme
1 tablespoon chopped chives
50g Parmesan, grated

1. Preheat the oven to 190°C/gas mark 5.

2. Heat a little olive oil in a large, deep saucepan and fry the onion until it is soft but not brown.

3. Put the stock in a saucepan over a medium heat.

4. Put the mushrooms on a baking tray, drizzle with a little olive oil and roast in the preheated oven for 15 minutes.

5. Add the garlic and rice to the onions and cook, stirring, for 2 minutes until the rice turns translucent. Pour in the wine and stir.

6. Add the warm stock one ladle at a time to the rice and stir until all the stock has been absorbed. Do this until the rice will take no more liquid. It should be moist but not runny. You may not need all the stock.

7. When the mushrooms are ready, add them to the rice and sprinkle in the thyme and chives.

8. Heat everything through, then serve immediately with the Parmesan on the side for sprinkling.

Chicken with Rice, Sage and Onion

SERVES 4–5

2 carrots, diced
1 large onion, sliced
80g frozen or fresh peas
80g frozen or fresh broad beans
4 tablespoons sage and onion stuffing mix
150g long-grain rice
1 whole chicken, about 2–2.5kg in weight
600ml water or chicken stock (see page 16)
Salt and pepper to taste

1. Preheat the oven to 190°C/gas mark 5.

2. Put the carrots, onion and other vegetables in a large casserole.

3. Add the stuffing mix and rice and place the chicken on top.

4. Pour in the stock or water and cover either with a lid or foil.

5. Cook for 30 minutes, then turn down the heat to 170°C/gas mark 3 and cook for 1½ hours. Halfway through the cooking time, check to see if the casserole needs any more liquid; if so, add a little more hot water around the chicken.

6. When the chicken is fully cooked, remove from the dish, carve all the meat from the bones and put it back in the casserole.

7. Heat for 10 minutes, then serve.

Lamb Rissoles

SERVES 4

Olive oil for frying
1 medium onion, finely chopped
1 garlic clove, chopped
½ teaspoon cumin
1 teaspoon paprika
225g minced lamb
1 tablespoon sweet chilli sauce
225g cooked rice
1 egg, beaten
15g flour
100g breadcrumbs

1. Heat the oil in a frying pan and fry the onion, garlic, cumin, paprika and lamb together for 5 minutes. Place in a bowl to cool.

2. When the meat is cold, stir in the sweet chilli sauce and the rice and combine with a little of the egg. Put the rest of the egg in a dish.

3. Flour your hands and form the mixture into rissole shapes. Put on a plate and transfer the rissoles to the fridge to chill for 20 minutes.

4. Dip each rissole in the beaten egg, then the breadcrumbs, and fry in hot oil on both sides. Alternatively, deep-fry them in a fat fryer or large pan.

5. Drain on kitchen paper and serve with a green salad and some homemade mayonnaise.

PASTA AND RICE DISHES

My Notes.

6
Pies and Pastry

The old saying 'Cold hands and a warm heart' describes the type of person who is good at making pastry. I have never met anyone with a cold heart and warm hands (!), but if yours do happen to be warm, simply cool them under running water and you will be able to make the best pastry in the world.

Making pastry of any kind is always worth doing, as it gives you a sense of achievement and you know exactly what goes in it. It is cheaper and you can make more than you need at any one time and freeze it for when time is short.

Shortcrust Pastry

This is the most widely used of all pastry recipes and can be made very quickly.

300g plain flour
½ level teaspoon salt
65g butter, cut into small pieces
65g lard, cut into small pieces
2 tablespoons cold water

1. Sift the flour and salt into a bowl; lift the sieve as high up as possible so that the flour gets a really good airing.

2. Add both the fats and begin to rub the fat into the flour. If you find halfway through that the fat softens too much, put the bowl into the fridge for 10 minutes.

3. Keep rubbing in until the mixture looks like breadcrumbs. Keep it light and if your hands get hot, run your wrists under cold water, dry them and keep going. This stage may be done in the food processor.

4. Add 1 tablespoon of water and mix in with a knife; the pastry should start to form clumps. Add the other tablespoon of water and keep mixing in with the knife.

5. Bring the pastry together with your hands as lightly and quickly as possible. Don't be tempted to knead it as it will end up tough and inedible.

6. When the dough forms a smooth ball, wrap it in cling film and put it in the fridge to cool for at least 30 minutes before use. When a recipe calls for half a quantity of the pastry, use half and freeze the other – or make something else with it.

Tips for successful shortcrust pastry

Keep all ingredients as cool as possible.

Cut the fat into small pieces and put it in the fridge again to cool.

Roll out the pastry quickly and to the thickness you desire. Too much rolling makes pastry heavy.

Make sure the fat is very cold, straight from the fridge, and that the water is ice-cold.

MAKES 24 SMALL TARTS

Jam Tart Bonanza

1 quantity of shortcrust pastry
Strawberry jam
Raspberry jam
Marmalade
Lemon curd

1. Preheat the oven to 190°C/gas mark 5. Butter 2 x 12-hole bun tins.

2. Roll out half of the pastry and cut out 12 circles with a medium-sized biscuit cutter.

3. Put each piece in the first bun tin and press down lightly to line each hole. Repeat with the other tin.

4. Put a teaspoon of jam or preserve into each pastry shell – use 6 of each type for a good variety.

5. Bake for 15 minutes, or until the pastry is golden brown. Cool for a few minutes in the tins, then transfer the tarts to a wire rack to cool completely.

Bakewell Tart

Half a quantity of shortcrust pastry
4 tablespoons jam of your choice
3 eggs
150g golden caster sugar
150g ground almonds
½ teaspoon almond extract or essence
150g butter
25g flaked almonds
Icing sugar for dusting

1. Preheat the oven to 190°C/gas mark 5.

2. Butter a deep 20cm pie dish or tin and line it with the pastry. Spread the jam over the entire area.

3. Whisk the eggs and sugar together in a bowl until thick and paler in colour.

4. Stir in the almonds and extract. Use a metal spoon, if you have one.

5. Melt the butter either in the microwave or in a pan over a very low heat. Pour into the almond mixture and mix well.

6. Pour the mixture over the pastry. Spread the flaked almonds over the top.

7. Bake in the preheated oven for 30–35 minutes until golden. Dust with icing sugar when cool.

Variation
If, like me, you like glacé cherries, then put 8–9 whole cherries evenly over the pie after spreading the jam over the pastry and before pouring over the topping.

Traditional Coconut Slice

Half a quantity shortcrust pastry
4 tablespoons raspberry jam
3 egg whites
80g caster sugar
150g desiccated coconut

1. Preheat the oven to 190°C/gas mark 5.

2. Butter an 18cm x 27cm rectangular tin and line it with the pastry quite thinly.

3. Spread the jam over the entire area.

4. Whisk the egg whites until they are light and foamy, but not stiff. Whisk in the sugar.

5. Stir in the coconut and spoon the mixture over the pastry.

6. Bake for 25–30 minutes, or until the top is golden. Cool before serving.

Strawberry and Kiwi Tart

Butter for greasing
Half a quantity of shortcrust pastry
250g small strawberries, hulled and halved
1 kiwi fruit, peeled and sliced thinly, then each slice halved

For the custard layer
250ml milk
2 tablespoons cornflour
3 egg yolks
2 tablespoons caster sugar
½ teaspoon vanilla extract

1. Preheat the oven to 190°C/gas mark 5.

2. Butter and line a deep 20cm pie or tart tin with pastry. Bake the pastry 'blind' by placing a circle of baking parchment at least 4cm bigger than the tin inside it and spread this with baking beans or dried beans. Bake in the preheated oven for 15 minutes.

3. Allow to cool while you make the custard. Put the milk, except for 3 tablespoons, in a saucepan and heat until it is warm. Remove from the heat.

4. Mix the reserved milk with the cornflour.

5. Whisk the egg yolks and sugar together in a bowl. Pour the warm milk into the egg mixture, whisking to combine, and stir in the vanilla.

6. Pour the custard back in the pan and stir in the cornflour paste. Mix in vigorously. Heat at a low temperature until the mixture comes to the boil, whisking all the time.

7. Allow to cool for 30 minutes. Put a disc of baking parchment over the custard to stop a skin forming on the top.

8. Spread the custard evenly over the pastry shell.

9 Arrange the strawberries on the custard in concentric circles, alternating with slices of kiwi fruit.

10 Refrigerate for 30–40 minutes before serving.

Serving suggestion
If you want a glossy finish to the tart, warm some apricot jam in a pan then brush it over the fruit with a pastry brush.

SERVES 8

Deep-filled Cheese and Onion Pie

This is a large pie and would serve 8 people.

- Butter for greasing
- 1 quantity of shortcrust pastry
- 200g red Leicester cheese, grated
- 200g mature Cheddar, grated
- 50g crumbly Cheshire cheese, crumbled or grated
- 1 large onion, very finely chopped
- 1 egg
- ½ teaspoon ground black pepper
- 1 level teaspoon mustard powder

1. Preheat the oven to 190°C/gas mark 5.

2. Butter a large, deep pie dish, roll out just over half of the pastry and use this to line the dish.

3. In a large bowl, mix all the cheeses together with the onion. Mix until fully combined.

4. Beat the egg and whisk in the pepper and mustard. Stir into the cheese mixture.

5. Pile the cheese mixture into the pastry shell, then roll out the lid. Dampen the edges with water and lay the lid carefully on top of the pie. Crimp or squeeze the edges together. Brush the top with egg and milk if you like a shiny finish.

6. Bake in the preheated oven for 35–45 minutes, or until the top is a deep golden colour.

7. Allow the pie to rest for 10 minutes before serving with baked beans or a salad.

SERVES 8

Pork, Sun-dried Tomato and Chicken Pie

This is best cooked in a round 20cm springform baking tin, as it is much easier to remove.

- Butter for greasing
- 1 quantity of shortcrust pastry
- 750g minced pork
- Salt and pepper to taste
- 1 x 200g jar sun-dried tomatoes in oil
- 500g uncooked chicken, either thinly sliced or diced

1. Preheat the oven to 170°C/gas mark 3.

2. Grease the tin well with butter. Roll out ⅔ of the pastry – not too thick but thick enough to hold together when cooked; about 4mm is a suitable thickness. Use this to line the tin.

3. Put the pork in a bowl and season with salt and pepper. Put this in the bottom of the pie and press down evenly.

4. Drain the tomatoes, reserving the oil for frying or as a salad dressing. Put a layer over the pork, overlapping the slices slightly.

5. Put the chicken meat on top of the tomatoes and season with a little salt and pepper if you wish.

6. Roll out the rest of the pastry to make the lid. Dampen the edges of the pastry base with water and lay the lid on top of the pie. Crimp the edges together with your finger and thumb. Make 3 slits in the top to allow the steam to escape.

7. Bake the pie for 2 hours, the first hour at 170°C/gas mark 3, the second hour at 160°C/gas mark 2–3. You will know when it is cooked by piercing the centre with a knife: it should slide in easily and there should be very little residue left on the blade.

8. Allow to cool for 30–40 minutes before serving warm, or allow to cool completely and put in the fridge for a few hours, then serve cold with salad.

SERVES 6

Bacon and Leek Pie

Butter for greasing
Half a quantity of shortcrust pastry
25g butter
100g smoked bacon, chopped
5 large leeks, sliced
Salt and black pepper to taste
1 tablespoon plain flour
150ml vegetable stock (see page 19)

1. Preheat the oven to 190°C/gas mark 5.

2. Butter a 20cm tin or pie dish.

3. Roll out just over half of the pastry and use this to line the base of the tin or pie dish.

4. Melt the butter in a frying pan and add the bacon. Fry for 1 minute, then add the leeks. Cook gently until the leeks are soft. Season to taste, remembering that bacon is salty.

5. Sprinkle in the flour and stir into the buttery juices.

6. Add the stock gradually – use just enough to cover the leeks and thicken when mixed with the flour. You may not need to use all the stock.

7. Cool for 5 minutes, then fill the pie with the leek mixture.

8. Roll out the rest of the pastry to make the lid. Dampen the edges of the pie with water and lay the lid on, securing the edges by pressing them together.

9. Glaze the pie top with a little beaten egg or milk if you wish, then bake for 30–40 minutes in the preheated oven.

10. Cool for 5 minutes before serving.

SERVES 6–8

Mushroom and Pepper Quiche

- Butter for greasing
- Oil for frying
- 1 small red and a green pepper, chopped
- 8 medium open-cup mushrooms, sliced
- Salt and black pepper to taste
- Half a quantity of shortcrust pastry
- 2 eggs
- 140ml of milk, or a mixture of milk and single cream
- 50g Parmesan

1. Preheat the oven to 190°C/gas mark 5. Butter a 20cm pie or flan tin.

2. Heat the oil in a saucepan and fry the peppers for 2–3 minutes. Add the mushrooms and fry until most of the mushroom liquid has evaporated. Season to taste.

3. Roll out the pastry and use it to line the tin. Bake the pastry 'blind' by placing a circle of baking parchment at least 4cm bigger than the tin inside it and spread this with baking beans or dried beans. Bake in the preheated oven for 10 minutes.

4. Put the peppers and mushrooms in the semi-cooked pastry shell, spreading them evenly over the base.

5. Whisk the eggs and milk together and pour over the vegetables.

6. Top with the grated Parmesan and bake for about 30–35 minutes, or until the egg mixture is set. Cool before serving hot, or refrigerate and serve cold.

Serving suggestion

This makes an excellent buffet party or picnic dish.

ROUGH PUFF PASTRY

Rough Puff Pastry

This is the only type of puff pastry I make. It is the quickest and easiest that I know of, and the result is still light and flaky pastry.

The amount this recipe makes is enough to cover 1 large pie, make 6 large apple turnovers or 12 sausage rolls.

225g plain flour
½ teaspoon salt
180g butter, straight from the fridge
80–100ml cold water

1. Sift the flour and salt into a bowl.

2. Add the butter in a whole block and cut it into the flour with a knife until the pieces are about 1cm in size. Alternatively, put the butter in the freezer for 1 hour, remove and grate, then stir into the flour.

3. Stir in the water and bring together with the knife. Only use your hands at the very last minute to make a soft dough.

4. Dust your work surface with flour and roll out the pastry into a rectangle about 3 times as long as it is wide.

5. Fold the top third over to the centre, then the bottom third over the top and seal the edges by pinching them together.

6. Turn the pastry so that one sealed edge is next to you and roll out into another rectangle. Fold and seal in the same way as above.

7. Do this twice more, then leave the pastry to rest for 30 minutes before using it in your recipe.

Recipe tip
Be very gentle with this pastry when rolling so as not to allow any of the air to escape.

SERVES 4–5

Steak and Kidney Pie

- 2 tablespoons sunflower oil for frying
- 1 large onion, sliced
- 800g steak and kidney, diced
- About 280ml beef stock (see page 17)
- 10 mushrooms, halved
- 4 anchovy fillets in oil, drained
- 1 tablespoon plain flour mixed with 2 tablespoons water
- 1 quantity of rough puff pastry

1. Heat the oil in a lidded saucepan and fry the onion until tender, then add the steak and kidney and pour over the stock. Simmer for 1 hour and 10 minutes.

2. Add the mushrooms and anchovy fillets and simmer 20 minutes more.

3. Stir in the flour paste and mix well into the gravy. Boil for 2 minutes, then remove from the heat.

4. Preheat the oven to 190°C/gas mark 5.

5. Pour the meat into a deep pie dish and roll out the pastry to fit the top.

6. Place the pastry on top of the meat and bake immediately for 25 minutes until the pastry has risen and is golden brown.

7. Serve immediately with boiled potatoes and buttered carrots.

Oriental Sausage Rolls

MAKES 12 GOOD-SIZED ROLLS

These make a change from ordinary sausage rolls.

- 500g minced pork
- 2 garlic cloves, chopped
- 1 tablespoon oyster sauce
- 3 teaspoons soy sauce
- ½ teaspoon five-spice powder
- 1 quantity of rough puff pastry

1. Preheat the oven to 200°C/gas mark 6.

2. Combine all the ingredients, except the pastry, in a bowl and use your hands to massage the garlic and flavourings into the meat.

3. Roll out the pastry until it measures about 30cm square.

4. Divide the pork mixture into 3 equal sections and roll each into 3 sausage shapes the length of the pastry.

5. Cut the pastry into 3 sections and place a sausage down each one. Brush the edges with a little water. Fold the pastry over and press the edges together to seal. Cut each sausage shape into 4 sections and place on a greased baking sheet.

6. Brush with egg or milk if you wish and bake for 25–30 minutes, or until golden brown.

MAKES 4 LARGE OR 8 SMALL TURNOVERS

- 2 Bramley apples, peeled, cored and diced
- 1 tablespoon honey
- 50ml apple juice
- Juice of 1 lemon
- 1 quantity of rough puff pastry
- 2 Granny Smith apples, cored, peeled and sliced
- A little brown sugar for topping

1. Preheat the oven to 200°C/gas mark 6.

2. Stew the Bramleys in the honey, apple juice and lemon juice until they 'fall' into a sauce. Cool.

3. Roll out the puff pastry and cut into 4 large squares or 8 small ones.

4. Put a spoonful of the stewed apple onto each square and top with 3–4 Granny Smith apple slices.

5. Moisten the edges of the squares with water and fold into triangles. Pinch to seal well and place on a greased baking sheet.

6. Bake for 15–20 minutes, or until well risen and golden. Remove from the oven and dust with brown sugar. Cool before serving.

Serving suggestion
Serve hot or cold with custard or cream.

HOT-WATER CRUST PASTRY

Hot-water Crust Pastry

This type of pastry is traditionally used to make a raised crusted pie, such as the pork pie below.

500g plain flour
1 level teaspoon salt
220ml boiling water
220g lard

1. Sieve the flour and salt together into a mixing bowl and make a well in the centre.

2. Pour the boiling water into a heatproof jug and add the lard. Allow it to dissolve into the water before stirring it into the flour with a wooden spoon.

3. Bring the pastry together with your hands to form a smooth, pliable dough. Cool before using.

Raised Pork Pie

Butter for greasing
1 quantity of hot-water crust pastry
500g minced pork
500g pork shoulder., cut into 1cm pieces, keeping a little of the fat on
2 level teaspoons salt
White pepper to taste

1. Preheat the oven to 175°C/gas mark 3. Grease a 20cm round loose-bottomed or springform tin.

2. Roll out the hot-water crust pastry to approximately 5mm thick and use it to line the tin. It should be slightly thicker than other pastry as it has to be cooked for longer.

3. Combine the two meats with the salt and pepper and stir well.

4. Press the meat down firmly into the pastry case and top with a pastry lid. Seal down the edges firmly by pinching them together, and brush with a beaten egg or milk glaze if you wish.

5. Place the tin on a baking sheet so as to catch any drips from the meat and bake for 1½ hours. Test the centre with a knife; it is cooked if it comes out clean. If not yet ready, cook for 15 minutes more.

6. Leave to cool in the tin, preferably overnight, and the juices will firm up, making the pie ready to slice.

Variations

To vary the flavour, try adding the following to the meat:

- ½ teaspoon sage
- a little grated nutmeg
- 1 teaspoon mustard powder
- ½ teaspoon celery salt

Suet Crust Pastry

This is the easiest of all the pastry recipes. It can be steamed or baked. When steamed, it is soft and light, and when baked, it is crisp and melts in the mouth.

This recipe makes enough pastry for a steak and kidney pudding made in an 850ml basin.

200g self-raising flour
½ level teaspoon salt
100g suet
Cold water to mix

1. Sieve the flour and salt together and stir in the suet.

2. Mix in the water, a teaspoon at a time, until the dough is soft but pliable.

3. Knead gently to bring the dough together and use in the recipe below.

Steak and Kidney Pudding

SERVES 5–6

Butter for greasing
1 quantity of suet crust pastry
750g best braising steak, cut into 1cm pieces
200g ox kidney, diced
30g flour seasoned with ¼ teaspoon salt and a pinch of black pepper
Oil for frying
1 medium onion
300ml beef stock (see page 17)

1. Grease an 850ml pudding basin.

2. Roll out two-thirds of the pastry to approximately 1cm thick and use it to line the basin.

3. Mix the meat and kidney with the seasoned flour and coat well.

4. Heat the oil in a saucepan and fry the onion until soft. Cool.

5. Put a layer of meat and kidney in the basin, then a layer of onions, then more meat. Keep layering until you finish with a layer of onions.

6. Pour in enough of the stock until you can just see it.

7. Roll out the rest of the pastry to make the lid and stick it down around the edges.

8. Cover the basin with 2 layers of greaseproof paper and tie securely with string. If you make a fold in the paper, it will allow for the pudding to rise.

9. Stand the basin in a large pan of hot water that reaches halfway up the sides. Bring to the boil and boil for 2½ hours. Alternatively, cook in a steamer.

10. Serve hot with mashed potatoes, swede and carrots.

CHOUX PASTRY

SERVES 6

Choux Pastry

Chocolate eclairs and profiteroles are just some of the things you can make with this type of pastry.

70g plain flour
150ml water
50g butter
2 eggs

1. Sieve the flour into a bowl.

2. Put the water and butter into a saucepan and heat gently until the butter melts.

3. Bring to the boil, then remove from the heat and stir in the flour quickly with a wooden spoon.

4. Return the pan to the heat and cook for a 2–3 minutes, stirring all the time, until the mixture comes away from the sides.

5. Cool for 2 minutes, then gradually beat in the eggs. The dough should be thick enough for piping but not too stiff. Use immediately in your recipes – such as the chocolate eclairs on the next page.

MAKES 12 LARGE CAKES

Chocolate Eclairs

Butter for greasing
1 quantity choux pastry
150ml whipping cream, whipped until just thick enough to stand up in soft peaks

For eclairs only: the chocolate topping
50g dark chocolate
50g icing sugar mixed with a few teaspoons cold water to make firm icing
a knob of butter

For profiteroles only: the chocolate topping
100g dark chocolate
30g butter
30ml double cream

1. Preheat the oven to 200°C/gas mark 6. Grease a baking sheet.

2. Put the choux dough into a piping bag and pipe strips about 8cm long onto the baking sheet. Drizzle the strips with a little water to help them rise. Bake for 20 minutes until puffed up and well risen.

3. Remove from the oven and release the steam inside the pastries by piercing each with a darning needle. They will then stay crisp.

4. Cut in half lengthways and fill with the whipped cream.

5. Melt the chocolate in a bowl over a pan of hot water, then mix in the icing sugar along with a knob of butter.

6. Spread chocolate icing on each eclair.

These will only keep for 24 hours – *if* they last that long!

To make profiteroles

1. Preheat the oven to 200°C/gas mark 6. Grease a baking sheet.

2. Pipe small blobs of the pastry onto the baking sheet and bake for 15 minutes.

3. Either split the profiteroles in half or use a cooking syringe to insert the cream into the centre of the choux puffs.

4. Pile them up on a serving plate and drizzle with the chocolate topping below.

For the chocolate topping

1. Put all the ingredients in a bowl over some hot water and stir gently until all the chocolate has melted.

2. Use this to drizzle over the mountain of profiteroles.

My Notes

7

Take-away and Restaurant-style Meals

It is wonderful to go out to eat or send out for a meal – of that there is no doubt. Yet it is also a great pleasure to eat in, and it is certainly easier on your purse if you make at least some of the items on the 'treat menu' for yourself. The problem comes in deciding what to have. When Josh wants a pizza, Rebecca wants a Chinese, and Paul and I want a curry, there are such negotiations you'd think it was the United Nations! Preparation is the key here – as is a good supply of herbs and spices, which make up the bulk of the cost.

ITALIAN

MAKES 2 DEEP-BASE 23–25CM PIZZAS

These are most people's favourite take-aways and are certainly very popular with my family.

For the basic dough
Oil for greasing
700g strong white flour
2 teaspoons salt
1 x 7g sachet fast-action dried yeast
380–400ml warm water
1 tablespoon olive oil

1. Preheat the oven to its hottest setting. Oil 2 pizza tins or 2 large baking sheets.

2. Sieve the flour and salt together in a bowl. Stir in the dried yeast.

3. Add half of the water and the olive oil and mix in with a wooden spoon.

4. Add more water and start to combine the dough with your hands. Add more water to make a pliable, soft dough, then knead on a floured surface for 10 minutes.

5. Leave to prove for 20 minutes; any longer and the dough won't roll out easily.

6. Divide the dough into 2 equal pieces and press and stretch it to fit the pans, or form into a rough pizza shape. Roll out to finish off the shaping.

7. Top with your favourite ingredients and bake in a very hot oven (230°C/gas mark 8) for 10–15 minutes.

Tomato Pizza Topping

SUFFICIENT FOR A THICK TOPPING FOR 2 LARGE PIZZAS

150ml passata
1 garlic clove, grated
2 tablespoons tomato purée
A little salt
Herbs if you wish: try ½ teaspoon marjoram or thyme

1. Use a spoon to mix all the ingredients together in a jug or bowl. Spread the sauce over your pizza bases, then add the topping(s) of your choice.

Topping ideas

- A mixture of strong grated Cheddar and chunks of mozzarella cheese
- Tuna, prawns and anchovies
- Tuna with anchovies and black olives
- Thinly sliced chorizo sausage and salami scattered with sun-dried tomatoes
- Finely chopped spring onions, sliced red and green peppers and thinly sliced chestnut mushrooms
- Thinly sliced chicken tikka pieces and fresh halved cherry tomatoes

SERVES 4–5

Simple Lasagne

If your ragu sauce is already hot, then this lasagne only takes about 30–40 minutes to cook. If the sauce is cold, it will take about an hour.

1 quantity of ragu sauce, (see page 81)
16–18 sheets of lasagne

For the white sauce
425ml milk
2 level tablespoons cornflour
Salt and black pepper to taste
150g cheese, a mixture of Cheddar and Parmesan or any type

Preheat the oven to 200°C/gas mark 6.

To make the cheese sauce
1. In a heatproof bowl or jug, mix 3 tablespoons of the milk with the cornflour to make a paste.

2. Heat the rest of the milk until hot, then whisk it into the cornflour mixture.

3. Pour the mixture back into the pan over a low heat. Stir with a wooden spoon until it boils and thickens. Season to taste and stir in half of the cheese.

To make the lasagne
1. Put a ladle of ragu sauce in the bottom of a large, ovenproof dish or roasting pan, then add a layer of lasagne.

2. Carry on layering sauce then lasagne and finish with a layer of lasagne,

3. Pour over the sauce and sprinkle the top with the rest of the cheese.

4. Bake in the preheated oven for 30 minutes to 1 hour, depending on the heat of the ragu sauce.

5. Leave to settle in the pan for 5 minutes before serving.

Serving suggestion
The ragu and cheese sauce also makes a tasty cannelloni. Fill tubes of cannelloni pasta with some of the sauce (allow 2–3 tubes per person) and place in an ovenproof tin. Pour the rest of the sauce over the cannelloni, top with the cheese sauce, and bake the cannelloni at 200°C/gas mark 6 for 45 minutes.

INDIAN-STYLE DISHES

It is good to have a stock of spices and herbs for making Indian-style food; you can then make many tasty recipes. I recommend the following:

- Ground cumin and seeds
- Ground turmeric
- Cardamom pods
- Chilli powder or flakes
- Garam masala
- Fresh and ground ginger
- Ground coriander and seeds
- Ground cinnamon
- Cloves
- Dried methi/fenugreek leaves
- Madras curry powder

Chicken Korma

SERVES 6–8

1 small onion, chopped
Large knob of butter
4 garlic cloves, chopped
1 level teaspoon each of garam masala, ground cumin, ground coriander and turmeric
2cm piece of fresh ginger, grated
3 chicken breasts or 6 chicken thighs, chopped into 2cm pieces
200ml chicken stock (see page 16)
2 tablespoons ground almonds
Salt to taste
300ml warm water mixed with 4 tablespoons coconut milk powder
2 tablespoons double cream
Flaked almonds to decorate the top

1. Sauté the onion in the butter for a few minutes. Add the garlic, spices and fresh ginger and stir to mix well.
2. Add the chicken pieces and continue to cook for 10 minutes on a low heat.
3. Pour in the chicken stock and stir in the ground almonds.
4. Season with salt if necessary and simmer for 15 minutes.
5. Add the coconut milk and simmer for 5 minutes.
6. Stir in the cream and scatter with the flaked almonds to serve.
7. Serve with boiled rice and naan bread.

SERVES 3–4

Chicken Tikka Masala

3 chicken breasts, cut into bite-sized pieces
Juice of 1 lemon
2 teaspoons paprika
½ teaspoon chilli powder
½ teaspoon each of ground cumin, coriander and turmeric
1 teaspoon dried methi/fenugreek leaves
A little salt
150ml natural yoghurt, (don't use the low-fat variety as it will split during cooking)

For the sauce
25g butter
1 medium onion, chopped finely
3 garlic cloves, chopped
1 teaspoon madras curry powder
2cm piece of fresh ginger, grated
1 tablespoon tomato purée
2 ripe tomatoes, chopped
200ml passata
2 tablespoons chopped coriander leaves

1. Put the chicken pieces in a bowl and pour over the lemon juice, spices and salt to taste.

2. Stir in the yoghurt and leave to marinate for 3–4 hours.

3. If the chicken is in the fridge, remove it an hour before cooking or else it will be tough.

4. To make the sauce, heat the butter in a frying pan and fry the onion gently until soft.

5. Add the garlic, curry powder, ginger and tomato purée and stir well.

6. After a few minutes add the chicken and the tomatoes and cook for 10 minutes.

7. Add the passata and simmer for 10 more minutes.

8. Stir in the coriander leaves and serve with rice or naan bread (see page 113).

SERVES 3–4

Vegetable Madras

I large knob butter
I large onion, chopped
2 carrots, finely diced
I courgette, chopped
I red pepper, chopped
4 cauliflower florets, halved
50g peas
50g green beans, sliced
3 garlic cloves, chopped
3 dessertspoons madras curry powder
I teaspoon salt
8 medium mushrooms, halved
400g canned chopped tomatoes
A handful of fresh spinach or 4 portions of frozen

1. Melt the butter in a large pan and add the onion, carrots, courgette, peppers, cauliflower, peas and beans. Stir to coat in the butter and leave covered on a low heat for 15 minutes, stirring occasionally. The vegetables will sweat in the butter and release their juices to make a stock.

2. Add the garlic and madras powder and sweat for 5 more minutes.

3. Add the salt, mushrooms and tomatoes (if using frozen spinach, add this now) and simmer for 15 minutes, or until the carrots are tender.

4. Add the fresh spinach and cook for 3 minutes.

Serving suggestion
Serve with pilau rice and mango chutney.

Lamb Rogan Josh

SERVES 3–4

25g butter
I medium onion, sliced
I teaspoon each of ground cumin, coriander, turmeric and garam masala
I level teaspoon chilli flakes
2 garlic cloves, chopped
2cm fresh ginger, grated
750g diced lamb
400g canned tomatoes
I tablespoon tomato purée
Salt to taste
3 fresh tomatoes, quartered
4 tablespoons plain yoghurt

1. Preheat the oven to 180°C/gas mark 4.

2. Melt the butter in a pan and add the onion. Fry for 3–4 minutes, then add the spices, garlic and ginger.

3. Add the lamb and cook until the meat has browned a little.

4. Transfer the meat mixture to a lidded casserole dish and stir in the canned tomatoes and purée.

5. Season to taste, cover and put in the oven for 45 minutes.

6. Lift out the casserole and add the fresh tomatoes, pressing them down into the meat. Cover and put back in the oven for 25 minutes.

7. Stir in the yoghurt just before serving.

Pilau Rice

SERVES 3–4

25g butter
1 small onion, chopped finely
½ teaspoon cumin seeds
4 cardamom pods
4 cloves
400g long-grain or basmati rice
500ml chicken or vegetable stock (see pages 16 and 19)

1. Melt the butter in a large pan and add the onion. Cook until soft.

2. Stir in the spices and add the rice. Cook gently for 1 minute.

3. Add the stock and raise the heat to simmering. Cook until the rice has absorbed all the liquid. If the rice still isn't tender after adding all the stock, pour in a little hot water and continue to simmer.

4. Remove the cloves and cardamom pods before serving.

Naan Bread

MAKES 3

225g strong white flour
½ teaspoon salt
1 sachet fast-action yeast
4 tablespoons warm milk
1 tablespoon sunflower oil
2 tablespoons plain yoghurt
1 egg, beaten

Oil for greasing

1. Sieve the flour and salt together into a bowl and stir in the yeast.

2. Mix in the other ingredients and bring together with your hands.

3. Knead for 5 minutes, then leave in a warm place to double in size. This will take about 30–40 minutes.

4. Heat the oven to its highest temperature and heat some oil on a baking tray for 5 minutes.

5. Divide the dough into 3 pieces and roll out each piece into a teardrop shape.

6. Remove the baking tray from the oven and lay each naan on the hot tray. Bake immediately for 4–5 minutes, or until they have ballooned and started to turn golden brown.

7. Serve warm.

ORIENTAL-STYLE DISHES

Add the following to your store-cupboard so that you will be prepared whenever you want to make Chinese and oriental dishes.

- Dark soy sauce
- Oyster sauce
- Hoisin sauce
- Five-spice powder
- Sesame oil
- Rice wine

Chinese Barbecued Ribs

1kg pork ribs (ask the butcher to cut them up if you don't have a chopper)
4 tablespoons hoisin sauce
3 tablespoons honey
3 tablespoons water
3 tablespoons rice wine
2 tablespoons soy sauce
2 garlic cloves, chopped

1. Steam the ribs for 20 minutes. If you don't have a steamer or don't want to steam the ribs first, put them straight into the marinade (see below), but increase the cooking time to 1¼ hours.

2. Combine all the other ingredients in a bowl.

3. Cool the ribs for 10 minutes after steaming, then place them in the marinade and leave for 1 hour in a refrigerator.

4. Place the ribs in a roasting pan with all of the marinade, cover with foil and cook for 30 minutes at 190°C/gas mark 5.

5. Serve immediately.

Char Siu

Chinese roast pork can be eaten on its own or added to sauces such as oyster or black bean.

500g pork fillet
2 tablespoons hoisin sauce
2cm piece of fresh ginger, grated
½ teaspoon five-spice powder
2 garlic cloves, grated
4 tablespoons honey
1 tablespoon soft brown sugar
2 tablespoons yellow bean sauce
2 tablespoons soy sauce
30ml rice wine

1. Place the pork in a dish and cut slashes into the meat all along the upper part. Avoid cutting right through, however.

2. Combine all the other ingredients in a bowl and stir to blend.

3. Pour the marinade over the pork and rub it into the meat with the back of a spoon.

4. Leave for 3–4 hours in a cool place.

5. Preheat the oven to 190°C/gas mark 5.

6. Place the pork on a rack over a roasting tin half-filled with boiling water. Reserve the marinade for use halfway through the roasting.

7. Roast the pork for 20 minutes, then baste the meat with the marinade, and continue roasting for another 20 minutes.

8. When cooked, allow to stand away from the water, then slice the meat into strips.

9. Serve with cooked medium-sized noodles and a little soy sauce.

SERVES 3–4

Vegetable Chow Mein

- 1 tablespoon sunflower oil and 2 teaspoons sesame oil
- 1 onion, chopped
- 2 garlic cloves, chopped
- 1 red pepper, thinly sliced
- 50g mangetout
- 4–5 nests dried noodles or 400g fresh noodles
- 1 carrot, grated
- 50g chestnut mushrooms, sliced
- 80g bean sprouts
- 2 tablespoons each of rice wine and oyster sauce, mixed together

1. Heat the oils in a frying pan or wok and add the onion and garlic. Fry for 3–4 minutes.

2. Add the pepper and mangetout and fry for 4 minutes.

3. Meanwhile, cook the noodles according to the instructions on the packet. Drain and leave in a colander until needed.

4. Stir in the grated carrots and mushrooms and fry for 2–3 minutes.

5. Add the bean sprouts and rice wine and oyster sauce mix and stir.

6. Stir in the cooked noodles and heat through.

7. Serve immediately.

SERVES 3–4

Special Fried Rice

This may be served as a meal in itself, or as an accompaniment to other dishes.

2 tablespoons sunflower oil
1 teaspoon sesame oil
2 garlic cloves, chopped
1 teaspoon grated ginger
2 spring onions, finely chopped
450g (dried weight) long-grain rice cooked according to the packet instructions
50g peas, cooked
Salt to taste
110g prawns
250g *char siu*, sliced (see page 115)
2 tablespoons soy sauce
2 eggs, beaten

1. Heat a wok or large frying pan containing both the sunflower and sesame oils.

2. Add the garlic, ginger and spring onions.

3. Add the rice and peas and season with a little salt.

4. Stir in the prawns and *char siu* and add the soy sauce.

5. Stir in the eggs and allow them to set before stirring them into the rice mixture.

6. Serve with extra soy sauce or some oyster sauce.

ORIENTAL-STYLE DISHES

Kebabs with Sweet Chilli Sauce

I make these into small, round patties, but you can press the mixture onto skewers. They are delicious served with a sweet chilli sauce.

500g minced lamb
1 teaspoon dried mint
1 teaspoon ground cumin
2 garlic cloves, finely chopped
½ level teaspoon chilli powder
1 small onion, finely grated
1 level teaspoon salt

1. Combine the meat and all the other ingredients together in a mixing bowl.

2. Dampen your hands with water and form the mixture into round patties or squeeze onto skewers into sausage shapes.

3. Cook on a lightly oiled baking sheet in a hot oven for 20–25 minutes, or on the barbecue until cooked.

4. Serve with sweet chilli sauce (below).

Sweet Chilli Sauce

3 garlic cloves
3 red chilli peppers
2 green chilli peppers
2 tablespoons honey
2 tablespoons cider vinegar

1. Put all the ingredients into a food processor and whiz until you have a coarse paste.

2. Add a little more cider vinegar to loosen if too stiff.

3. Serve with the kebabs.

THE BURGER BAR

Homemade burgers are the best. You know exactly what has gone into them and they are easy to make. Simply use good, lean mince beef and some seasoning.

Burgers

MAKES 4 LARGE OR 6 SMALL BURGERS

- 500g lean minced beef or steak
- 1 tablespoon tomato purée
- 1 teaspoon paprika
- 1 level teaspoon salt

1. Combine all the ingredients in a bowl and mix well with your hands.

2. Use food rings, if you have them, to form your burgers, then remove the ring and press down with your hand. They will keep their shape if you do this carefully. If you don't have any rings, just form the mixture into patties with your hands.

3. Fry or grill them on both sides for 3–4 minutes. Serve in buns with a salad and the tomato relish below.

Tomato Relish

- 250g tomatoes, chopped
- 2 red peppers, chopped finely
- 1 large onion, chopped very finely
- ½ teaspoon chilli flakes
- 200g soft brown sugar
- 200ml white vinegar

1. Put all the ingredients in a pan on a low heat, stirring until all the sugar has dissolved.

2. Raise the heat and bring to the boil. Turn the heat down to a simmer and cook for 25–30 minutes until thick.

3. Pot into a sterilised screw-topped 450g jam jar.

4. Serve when cool with the burgers.

Storage
This will keep for 3 months in the fridge.

SERVES 4

Southern-style Chicken

- ½ teaspoon chilli powder
- 1 teaspoon each cayenne pepper and paprika
- 600ml milk
- 6–8 chicken thighs, each cut into 2 pieces
- 250g plain flour
- ½ teaspoon each celery salt, garlic granules and ground black pepper
- ½ teaspoon each dried parsley and tarragon
- Salt to taste
- Oil for cooking

1. Whisk the chilli powder, cayenne and paprika into the milk. Place the chicken in the milk and leave to soak for 3–4 hours.

2. Sieve the flour into a bowl and stir in the celery salt, garlic granules, pepper and herbs. Add a little more table salt if you wish.

3. Grease a baking sheet with sufficient oil to coat the whole tray. Heat the oven to 200°C/gas mark 6.

4. Lift each piece of chicken out of the milk and shake off any excess liquid. Dip the chicken into the seasoned flour and coat well.

5. Place the chicken on the baking sheet and cook for 25–30 minutes, or until golden and crispy.

6. Serve with potato wedges (below).

Spicy Potato Wedges

SERVES 4

- 3–4 medium potatoes, each cut into 8 wedges
- ½ teaspoon cayenne pepper
- ½ teaspoon ground cumin
- Salt and black pepper to taste
- Sunflower or olive oil

1. Preheat the oven to 220°C/gas mark 7.

2. Put the potato wedges in a bowl and sprinkle over the spices. Season with salt and black pepper. Mix well.

3. Grease a baking sheet with sufficient oil to coat the whole tray and place the potatoes on the sheet.

4. Cook for 20–30 minutes until crispy.

My Notes

8

Salads, Dips and Mayonnaise

Given the chance, my husband, Paul, would live on salad. It's not that he's a vegetarian; he just loves salad and has invented every possible type of dressing, some of which, quite frankly, I find a little overpowering. But it's the little extras like dressing that make a salad work. The coleslaw you make yourself is not only cheaper, but it's amazingly flavoured, and the mayo recipe is just like a bit of culinary magic before your eyes. ('No, it's simple science.' – Paul.)

In this chapter are the salads you would buy in the coleslaw section of your supermarket, such as pasta, rice and couscous salads. They are quick to make yourself and, best of all, you can tailor the ingredients to your own taste. They can also add interest to a buffet party and make a plain green salad much more enjoyable. Unless otherwise stated, all the salad recipes in this chapter will serve 2–3 people as a side dish.

SALADS, DIPS AND MAYONNAISE

Many of these salads use mayonnaise as a staple ingredient. Here is a super-fast way to make your own. You will need to use a hand blender, but it is well worth buying one just to make this mayonnaise recipe. It will make enough to use in two different types of salad, and still have a bit left over for other uses.

Speedy Mayonnaise

180ml sunflower oil
1 full egg and 1 egg yolk
Pinch of salt
1 teaspoon lemon juice
¼ teaspoon English mustard

1. Put all the ingredients in a bowl or glass and whiz with a hand blender. Within 15 seconds you will have made your mayonnaise!

Coleslaw

Half a small onion, white or red
1 medium carrot, grated
¼ (approx) white cabbage, shredded
3 rounded tablespoons good mayonnaise

1. Chop the onion finely and mix it and the grated carrot together in a bowl.

2. Shred the cabbage as finely as you prefer and mix that into the carrot and onion.

3. Add the mayonnaise and stir well to combine.

4. Transfer to a serving dish and serve.

PASTA SALADS

Pasta salads are very easy and can be made fairly quickly. You can use any ingredients that you may have in the fridge, from fish to vegetables, chicken to dried fruit. I always use wholewheat pasta, but you can use ordinary.

Prawn Pasta Salad

150g wholewheat dried pasta
100g large, shelled precooked prawns
¼ chopped cucumber
Salt and black pepper to taste
2 tablespoons crème fraîche
2 rounded tablespoons mayonnaise
½ level teaspoon sweet paprika

1. Cook the pasta according to the packet instructions and cool in cold water. Leave to drain.

2. In a large bowl, mix the prawns and cucumber, salt and black pepper.

3. Mix the crème fraîche and mayonnaise together with the paprika.

4. Stir the cooked pasta into the prawns and cucumber.

5. Add the mayonnaise and crème fraîche to the pasta and stir well to combine.

6. Transfer to a serving dish. Sprinkle a little more paprika on top of the salad before serving.

Cheese and Pasta Salad

150g wholewheat pasta of your choice
2 tablespoons mayonnaise
2 tablespoons crème fraîche
50g Cheddar
1 tablespoon chopped chives

1. Cook the pasta according to the packet directions and place in a large bowl when cool.

2. Mix the mayonnaise and crème fraîche together.

3. Add the cheese and chives to the pasta.

4. Stir in the crème fraîche and mayonnaise mixture.

5. Transfer to a serving bowl and serve topped with extra chives.

Serving suggestion
Try adding a few olives for colour.

Mexican Pasta Salad

150g wholewheat pasta
Half a red pepper, chopped
Half a green pepper, chopped
4 tablespoons sweet chilli sauce
220g canned red kidney beans, drained well
Crème fraîche to serve

1. Cook the pasta according to the packet instructions and cool in cold water. Leave to drain.

2. Combine the pasta with all the ingredients, then transfer to a serving dish and serve with crème fraîche.

Serving suggestion
This is really good as an accompaniment to prawn fishcakes or egg and ham pie.

Variation
You can hot it up with a few slivers of a hot chilli – if you dare!

Couscous Salad

This is delicious served with steak, and precludes the need for potatoes or rice.

Olive oil for frying
2–3 shallots, chopped
1 red pepper, chopped
1 small courgette, chopped
2 garlic cloves, crushed
150g couscous, cooked according to the packet instructions
2 tablespoons chopped fresh parsley
1 level teaspoon fresh thyme leaves
Salt and pepper to taste

1. Heat the oil in a frying pan and fry the shallots lightly.

2. Add the pepper, courgette and garlic and fry until tender.

3. Remove from the pan and allow to cool.

4. Once cool, mix the vegetables with the couscous and finely chopped herbs. Add salt and pepper to taste.

5. Serve with a mixture of virgin olive oil and balsamic vinegar.

RICE SALADS

Rice salads are easy to make and can serve as a colourful accompaniment or even as a main meal. Both these recipes use 150g of cooked, cooled rice, which can be either white or brown. Besides these recipes, you can use many other ingredients to make rice salads, such as chopped cooked mushrooms and crispy bacon, drained can of kidney beans and some chilli flakes, or cooked peas, prawns and chorizo sausage. The first recipe is one I adapted from a favourite kedgeree recipe.

Kedgeree-style Salad

- 2 tablespoons olive oil
- 2 level teaspoons curry paste
- 185g canned tuna in brine, well-drained
- 3 tablespoons frozen peas, cooked
- 150g rice, cooked and cooled
- 2 hard-boiled eggs, chopped
- Chopped parsley to decorate

1. Pour the oil into a saucepan and stir in the curry paste. Heat gently, then add the tuna and peas and stir to coat them with the spicy oil.

2. Remove from the heat and add the rice and eggs. Stir well and transfer to a serving dish.

3. Serve with chopped parsley sprinkled over the top of the salad.

Chicken and Rice Salad

This salad is great for using up any leftover chicken from a previous meal.

- 150g rice, cooked and cooled
- 100g chopped cooked chicken
- 2 tablespoons sweetcorn
- ½ red pepper, chopped
- ¼ cucumber, cubed
- Salt and pepper to taste

1. In a large bowl, combine all ingredients and mix well.

2. Transfer to a serving dish and add a few chopped herbs if desired.

SALADS AND DIPS

Coronation Chicken

This can be used as an accompaniment but it's also delicious in sandwiches, layered with lettuce and cucumber, or in a baked potato. Use chicken left from a roast if you like.

Oil for frying
½ small onion
1 teaspoon curry paste
2 tablespoons lemon juice
3 tablespoons mayonnaise
1 tablespoon double cream
150g cooked chicken
5 finely chopped dried apricots
Salt and pepper to taste

1. Heat the oil in a frying pan and sauté the onion until tender.

2. Add the curry paste and lemon juice.

3. Leave to cool thoroughly, then add the mayonnaise and cream.

4. Mix in chopped chicken and apricots and season to taste.

Serving suggestion
Use sultanas or raisins as an alternative to apricots if you wish.

DIPS

Hummus

This is delicious serve with thin slices of crusty bread and olives.

175g chickpeas soaked in cold water overnight
2 garlic cloves, chopped
5 tablespoons tahini
40–50ml fresh lemon juice
60ml mild olive oil
Salt to taste

1. Drain the chickpeas and put them in a saucepan. Pour on enough boiling water to cover and simmer for 2–2½ hours.

2. Drain well and purée with the chopped garlic, either in a food processor or by mashing together with a fork.

3. Add the tahini and lemon juice and mix well, then add the olive oil gradually while mixing well. Season to taste and transfer to a serving dish.

Guacamole

3 ripe avocados
1 beef tomato, chopped
2 garlic cloves, chopped
1 tablespoon lime juice
Pinch of salt

1. Cut each avocado in half, remove the stone and scoop out the flesh.

2. Mash the avocados and add all the other ingredients together. Stir well and serve.

SIDE SALADS

Great with most dishes or on their own with some crusty bread.

Oriental Watercress Salad

- 120g canned water chestnuts
- 2 large bunches of watercress
- 200g fresh bean sprouts

For the dressing

- 2 teaspoons sesame seeds
- 1 tablespoon sunflower oil
- 1 teaspoon sesame oil
- Juice of 1 lemon
- 2 tablespoons soy sauce
- 2 teaspoons honey

1. Drain the water chestnuts and slice thinly.

2. Wash the watercress and bean sprouts and pat dry. Place in a salad bowl and add the water chestnuts.

3. To make the dressing, first dry-fry the sesame seeds in a pan for 2–3 minutes over a low heat. Put all the dressing ingredients into a separate bowl and whisk together.

4. Pour over the vegetables and serve immediately.

Chickpea and Orange Salad

- 1 little gem lettuce, shredded
- 1 large carrot, grated
- 2 tablespoons chopped unsalted peanuts
- 200g canned chickpeas, drained
- Juice of 2 oranges
- 2 tablespoons reduced-fat hummus

1. Mix the lettuce with half of the grated carrot and place in a salad bowl or on a plate.

2. Mix the rest of the carrot and chopped peanuts with the chickpeas and place on top of the lettuce.

3. Whisk the orange juice and hummus together and pour over the salad.

4. Serve immediately.

Crunchy Salad

A third of a white cabbage, shredded finely
2 carrots, grated
Half an iceberg lettuce, cut finely
5cm piece of cucumber, chopped

For the dressing
2 tablespoons lemon juice
Juice and zest of 1 lime
1 tablespoon olive oil
A pinch salt
Black pepper
½ teaspoon dried thyme

For the croutons
2 large slices wholemeal bread, cubed (no need to remove crusts)
50ml olive oil, plus extra for greasing
2 garlic cloves, grated
½ teaspoon salt

1. First, make the croutons. Put the bread cubes on a lightly oiled baking sheet. Whisk the oil, garlic and salt together and pour evenly over the bread; mix the cubes around with your hands.

2. Put in a hot oven for 15 minutes, or until the bread is crispy. Remove from the baking sheet and place on kitchen paper to mop up any excess oil.

3. Next, put all the salad vegetables together in a bowl and mix thoroughly.

4. Whisk all the dressing ingredients together and drizzle over the salad.

4. Toss in the croutons and serve immediately.

My Notes

9
Vegetable Accompaniments

You would have thought that Paul, my husband, loved his vegetables more than I do, especially when he brings them out of the garden with a long set of instructions about how to handle them, what to wash them in, how to prepare and cook them. Well, my answer to all this is 'Cook them yourself!' (He does, too.)

He's right to be picky, however: vegetable dishes can make all the difference to a meal. They make it more interesting by adding texture and flavour, so it is well worth spending time and thought on your vegetable accompaniments.

Dauphinoise Potatoes

SERVES 3–4

3 medium potatoes, peeled and partially boiled for 6 minutes
300ml double cream
2 tablespoons milk
1 garlic clove, chopped
Salt and black pepper to taste

Preheat the oven to 200°C/gas mark 6. Slice the potatoes thinly and layer them into a buttered ovenproof dish.

2. Put the cream, milk, garlic and salt and pepper into a saucepan. Heat to just boiling, then pour over the potatoes.

3. Bake for 20 minutes, then serve.

Serving suggestion
Add some chopped chives and/or some grated Cheddar.

Champ

SERVES 3–4

1kg potatoes suitable for mashing, peeled and cubed
4 tablespoons milk
25g butter
Salt and black pepper to taste
5 spring onions, chopped finely

1. Boil the potatoes until tender and mash with the milk and butter.

2. Season to taste and mix in the spring onion

Variations
• For Mustard Mash, replace the spring onions with 2 teaspoons of wholegrain mustard.

• For Horseradish Mash, add 1 tablespoon of freshly grated horseradish to the recipe.

Bubble and Squeak

SERVES 3–4

- A knob of butter
- 1 small onion, finely chopped
- 800g potatoes, boiled and mashed
- 250g cabbage, shredded and steamed
- Salt and pepper to taste
- Oil for frying

1. Heat the butter in a frying pan and cook the onion until soft, but not brown.

2. Combine the mashed potato and cabbage in a bowl and mix in the onions. Season to taste.

3. Form the potato mixture into rounds and fry in a little oil in a large frying pan. Alternatively, place the rounds on a lightly oiled baking sheet and bake at 200°C/gas mark 6 for 15–20 minutes.

Herby Potato Cubes

SERVES 3–4

- Oil for greasing
- 3 large potatoes, peeled and diced
- 1 teaspoon rosemary
- Salt and pepper to taste
- Freshly chopped parsley for decoration

1. Preheat the oven to 200°C/gas mark 6.

2. Oil a baking tray and heat it for 3–4 minutes in the preheated oven, then place the diced potato on the sheet, sprinkle with rosemary and season to taste.

3. Cook for 25 minutes, then sprinkle with the parsley to serve.

Steamed Broccoli and Baby Onions

SERVES 2–3

8 broccoli spears
180g baby onions, peeled
Salt and pepper to taste
A knob of butter

1. Place the vegetables in a steamer and cook for about 8 minutes.

2. Add salt and black pepper and serve with the butter.

Red Cabbage with Orange and Sultanas

SERVES 4

Half a medium head of red cabbage, shredded finely
30g sultanas
Zest and juice of 1 orange
Salt and black pepper

1. Steam the cabbage for 6–7 minutes until it is cooked but still has 'bite'. While still in the steamer, add the sultanas and orange zest.

2. Place in a warm serving dish, pour over the orange juice and season to taste. Stir and serve.

Carrot and Pepper with Onion Sauce

SERVES 4

For the sauce
A knob of butter
Half a small onion, chopped finely
285ml milk
1 tablespoon cornflour
Salt and pepper

For the vegetables
2 carrots, diced
1 yellow pepper, sliced
1 green pepper, sliced
Salt and pepper

1. To make the sauce, heat the butter in a frying pan and cook the onion very gently until soft. Pour in the milk, reserving 2 tablespoons. Mix these with the cornflour.

2. Heat the milk mixture to boiling and remove from the heat. Stir in the milk and cornflour paste and return to the heat. Season to taste.

3. Bring to the boil, stirring continuously and as soon as boiling point is reached, pour into a heatproof jug while you steam the vegetables.

4. Steam the carrots and pepper for 8–10 minutes until tender, then put into a buttered ovenproof dish. Season to taste.

5. Pour on the onion sauce and place in a medium oven (180–190°C/ gas mark 4–5) to warm through.

SERVES 4

Traditional Mushy Peas

- 250g dried marrowfat peas
- 2 teaspoons sodium bicarbonate
- Water for steeping and cooking the peas
- Seasoning, this must be done at the end of the cooking time as they remain hard otherwise

1. Put the peas in a large bowl and sprinkle with the sodium bicarbonate. Pour warm water over the peas, enough to cover them by 6cm to allow for swelling. Stir and leave overnight.

2. Drain the peas and put in a large saucepan. Pour in sufficient water to cover.

3. Bring to the boil, then turn down the heat and simmer for 20–25 minutes. The peas should break down and 'fall' into the liquid. Add a little more water if you like them very mushy. Season to taste at the end of cooking.

Creamed Parsnips

SERVES 6

These are delicious served with a roast dinner or a steak.

- 800g parsnips, peeled and cut into 2cm pieces
- Salt and black pepper to taste
- 100ml double cream
- A knob of butter
- 50g walnuts, chopped

1. Preheat the oven to 190°C/gas mark 5.

2. Steam the parsnips for 15 minutes, or until tender. Add salt and pepper when cooked.

3. Put the parsnips in a bowl and mash them well with the butter and cream. Transfer to an ovenproof dish and scatter the top with the walnuts.

4. Bake for 15–20 minutes in the preheated oven. Serve hot.

SERVES 6

Stuffed Tomatoes

I prefer to use beef tomatoes for this recipe, but any large tomatoes would do. Serve as a starter or as an accompaniment to a main course.

25g butter
1 medium onion, chopped finely
100g mushrooms, chopped
6 large tomatoes
100g fresh breadcrumbs (use your grater on the fine side)
3 tablespoons freshly grated Parmesan
2 tablespoons chopped fresh parsley
Salt and pepper
½ teaspoon paprika

1. Preheat the oven to 180°C/gas mark 4.

2. Melt the butter in a frying pan and fry the onions until soft. Add the mushrooms and fry for 2–3 minutes.

3. Slice the tops off the tomatoes and reserve. Scoop out the pulp, taking care not to break the outer shell. Put the pulp into a bowl.

4. Put the cooked onions and mushrooms in the bowl with the tomato pulp. Add the breadcrumbs, half the cheese, and the parsley. Mix well Season to taste.

5. Spoon the mixture into the tomato shells and pile as high as possible. Sprinkle with the rest of the cheese and paprika, then replace the tops.

6. Place in a buttered ovenproof dish and bake for 15–20 minutes.

SERVES 4–8

Ratatouille

This is a quick version of the dish and is delicious serve with roast bacon or good sausages.

2 courgettes, sliced into discs
1 medium red onion, sliced
1 red pepper, sliced
1 yellow pepper, sliced
1 medium aubergine, cut lengthways, then each half sliced
5 ripe tomatoes, quartered
2 tablespoons olive oil
Salt and black pepper to taste
3 garlic cloves, chopped

1. Preheat the oven to 180°C/gas mark 4.

2. Put all the vegetables in a roasting pan and drizzle well with olive oil. Use your hands to make sure everything is coated.

3. Sprinkle with salt and pepper and the chopped garlic.

4. Roast for 15–20 minutes.

SERVES 4

Stuffed Marrow

This is more of a supper dish than an accompaniment.

- 1 medium marrow
- 50g butter
- 1 onion, chopped
- 2 garlic cloves, chopped
- 250g minced beef
- 50g breadcrumbs
- 1 tablespoon chopped basil
- 200g canned chopped tomatoes
- Salt and pepper to taste

1. Preheat the oven to 180°C/gas mark 4.

2. Cut the marrow three-quarters of the way up rather than in half, and scoop out the seeds so you have a larger channel in which to contain the meat. The marrow should now have a boat shape.

3. Heat half the butter in a frying pan and fry the onion for 2–3 minutes. Add the garlic and minced beef and cook until the meat is brown.

4. Put the meat mixture into a heatproof bowl and add the breadcrumbs, basil and canned tomatoes. Season and stir well.

5. Fill the inside of the marrow with the meat filling and dot with the remaining butter.

6. Place in a roasting pan and cover with foil. Bake for 50 minutes to 1 hour, and serve hot.

VEGETABLE ACCOMPANIMENTS

My Notes

10

Puddings and Desserts

Almost everyone I know has a sweet tooth. I once had a Queen of Puddings (see page 146) 'stolen', and I eventually found the dish in the greenhouse, but no one has, as yet, confessed to the crime. I love it when people enjoy my food, but I was really *very* cross at the time!

Still, I suppose I can't blame them. There is nothing as comforting as a homemade pudding, either hot or cold – yet many people are afraid to have a go at making them. They shouldn't be afraid: these days, with a microwave you can make old-fashioned steamed puddings in a fraction of the time it used to take. And rice pudding is one of the easiest desserts there is – and the homemade version always tastes so much better than canned.

SERVES 4–6

Dried Fruit Crumble

500g mixed dried fruit: prunes, apples, apricots, pears and peaches
1 tablespoon soft brown sugar
½ teaspoon vanilla extract
50ml water
200ml apple juice

For the topping
250g plain flour
50g porridge oats
180g butter, at room temperature
180g unrefined caster sugar

1. Preheat the oven to 200°C/gas mark 6.

2. Put the fruit in a pan with the sugar, vanilla, water and apple juice. Bring to the boil, then turn down the heat and simmer for 10 minutes.

3. If the liquid is not thick enough, remove the fruit and put into an ovenproof dish, boil the juice until it thickens, and pour over the fruit.

4. To make the topping, sift the flour into a bowl and stir in the oats.

5. Rub in the butter, then stir in the sugar.

6. Sprinkle the topping over the fruit and put it in the oven for about 30 minutes, or until the top is golden brown.

Serving suggestion
Serve with custard, cream or ice cream.

Traditional Rice Pudding

SERVES 4

Boiling the rice with a little water for 5 minutes reduces the cooking time. You can put it in the oven as raw, uncooked rice, but this will add an extra hour to the cooking time.

55g short-grain/pudding rice
1 tablespoon butter
1 x 410g can evaporated milk, made up to 580ml with water (you can also use 580ml ordinary whole milk)
75g golden caster sugar
Grated nutmeg for the top

1. Preheat the oven to 170°C/gas mark 3. Put the rice in a saucepan and add enough water just to cover it. Bring to the boil and cook for 5 minutes.

2. Drain the rice well and put into an ovenproof dish. Add the butter and pour in the milk.

3. Stir in the sugar and sprinkle with a little nutmeg.

4. Bake in the preheated oven for 1½ hours, stirring at intervals to distribute the rice.

5. Serve with your favourite preserve – or simply on its own.

SERVES 4–6

Chocolate Pudding with its Own Sauce

- 150g butter, plus extra for greasing
- 150g unrefined caster sugar
- 150g self-raising flour
- 2 eggs
- 5 tablespoons double cream
- 100g dark chocolate, broken into small chunks
- 2 tablespoons cocoa powder

1. Cream the butter and the sugar together. Add a tablespoon of flour and beat in the eggs.

2. Stir in 2 tablespoons of the cream and half the chocolate chunks.

3. Sift the cocoa and the rest of the flour into the creamed mixture. Fold in carefully.

4. Butter a pudding dish and put the rest of the chocolate and cream at the bottom of the basin.

5. Pour the pudding mixture on top of the chocolate and cream and level it out with the back of a spoon.

6. Either bake for 25–30 minutes at 180°C/gas mark 4, until springy to the touch, or cover with cling film and microwave for 3–5 minutes, until the pudding rises to meet the film.

7. Serve on its own or with the creamy white sauce below.

Creamy White Sauce

- 580ml whole milk
- 2 level tablespoons cornflour
- 2 level tablespoons sugar
- A knob of unsalted butter

1. Pour the milk into a saucepan, reserving 4 tablespoons.

2. Meanwhile, mix the cornflour and sugar together with the 4 tablespoons of milk until smooth. This can be done very easily in a small jam jar with a screw-top lid: put the milk mixture in the jar and screw on the lid tightly. Shake well and it's ready to use.

3. Heat the milk in the pan to almost boiling. Remove from the heat and whisk the cornflour mixture into the hot milk. Put back on a medium heat and stir constantly until the sauce boils.

4. Remove from the heat and stir in the knob of butter.

SERVES 4

Queen of Puddings

This is an easy dessert that uses up any stale cake you might have lurking in the cupboard. Traditionally it was made with breadcrumbs, but this variation tastes better and is economical to make.

Butter for greasing
Approximately 200g of any plain cake
3 eggs
300ml milk
1 tablespoon caster sugar
3–4 tablespoons strawberry or raspberry jam

1. Preheat the oven to 180°C/gas mark 4.

2. Butter an ovenproof dish and crumble the cake evenly over the bottom.

3. Separate 2 of the eggs, putting the whites into a grease-free bowl and the yolks into a jug. Add the other whole egg to the yolks and add the milk. Whisk them together with a fork and pour over the cake. Use a fork to squash the cake into the egg-and-milk mixture.

4. Bake for 30 minutes in the preheated oven, or until the mixture is firm.

5. Meanwhile, whisk the egg whites until they form stiff peaks, then fold in the sugar carefully with a metal spoon.

6. When the cake layer is cooked, spread the jam evenly over the top and pile on the meringue. Smooth it to the edges of the dish and put back in the oven for about 15 minutes to brown the meringue peaks lightly. Turn off the heat and let the meringue dry out for 10 minutes in the cooling oven.

7. Allow to stand for 20–25 minutes before serving warm with cream.

Stuffed Baked Apples

SERVES 4

Butter for greasing
4 Bramley apples, washed well, cores removed
100g mixed dried fruit: raisins, sultanas, currants, chopped apricots, etc.
2 tablespoons mincemeat
A knob of butter for each apple
50g soft brown sugar

1. Preheat the oven to 180°C/gas mark 4. Put the apples in a buttered ovenproof dish.

2. Combine the dried fruit and mincemeat together and push down into the cavity of the apples. fill each apple generously.

3. Put a knob of butter on top of each apple and sprinkle with the sugar.

4. Bake in the oven for 40–45 minutes.

Variation
Pour a glass of sherry over the apples before cooking.

SERVES 4

Fruit Sponge Puddings

This recipe can be adapted to use any fruit in season, such as gooseberries, blackberries, apples, damsons or plums.

80g butter, at room temperature
80g golden caster sugar
100g self-raising flour
1 egg, beaten
2 tablespoons milk
450g fruit in season, prepared in the following way:

Apples: peel, core and slice thinly, place in a buttered ovenproof dish. Sprinkle with a little brown sugar or honey.

Blackberries: wash well and put the fruit straight into a buttered ovenproof dish. Sprinkle with a little brown sugar to taste.

Damsons and plums: wash, halve and stone and then place in a buttered ovenproof dish. Sprinkle with 1 tablespoon brown sugar or honey.

Gooseberries: wash, top and tail them, then put in a pan together with 50g brown sugar or 2 tablespoons honey. Heat gently until the fruit simmers, then put in a buttered ovenproof dish.

Rhubarb: OK, yes, it's technically a vegetable, not a fruit, but it works like a fruit in this and other recipes! Wash and slice the stalks into 2cm pieces. For a soft texture, simmer in the same way as the gooseberries before arranging in the dish. Otherwise, place it in the buttered dish and sprinkle with 2 tablespoons brown sugar or honey.

To make the sponge topping

1. Preheat the oven to 180°C/gas mark 4.

2. Cream the butter and sugar together until light and fluffy.

3. Sift a tablespoon of the flour into the creamed mixture and beat in the egg.

4. Add the rest of the flour and fold in with a metal spoon.

5. Stir in the milk and spread the mixture over the prepared fruit.

6. Bake in the preheated oven for 45 minutes, or until the top of the sponge is springy to the touch.

7. Serve hot with cream or custard.

'STEAMED' SUET PUDDINGS

Microwaved suet puddings are both easy and quick to make. So long as you have the ingredients in your cupboard, you can decide to make one and have it ready to serve in about 15 minutes. I use vegetarian suet because it contains half the fat of the original suet and tastes good in a pudding recipe.

Once microwaved, the puddings need to stand for 2 minutes before removing the film. This allows any moisture in the pudding to settle while it continues to cook away from the oven.

Syrup Pudding

SERVES 4

Butter for greasing
4 tablespoons golden syrup
100g self-raising flour
50g vegetarian suet
50g golden caster sugar
2 eggs
1 teaspoon vanilla extract
4 tablespoons milk

1. Butter a 1.2-litre pudding basin and put the golden syrup in the bottom.

2. Sift the flour into a mixing bowl and stir in the suet and sugar.

3. Beat the eggs and vanilla into the milk and stir into the flour mixture with a fork. Work the liquid in briskly.

4. Spoon into the basin and cover with cling film. Pierce the film in the centre with the point of a knife.

5. Cook in the microwave at full power for 4–4½ minutes. The pudding should reach the cling film; this is an indication of it being ready. Remove from the oven and allow to stand for 2 minutes before removing the film.

6. Turn out onto a plate if you wish and serve with custard or cream.

Variations
Instead of golden syrup, try:
- 3 tablespoons orange marmalade
- 3–4 tablespoons jam
- 4 tablespoons lemon curd
- 3 tablespoons honey

'STEAMED' SUET PUDDINGS

SERVES 4

Chocolate Pudding

Butter for greasing
100g self-raising flour
2 tablespoons cocoa powder
70g golden caster sugar
50g vegetarian suet
2 eggs
4 tablespoons milk
50g dark chocolate, broken into small pieces

1. Butter a 1.2-litre pudding basin. Sift the flour and cocoa powder together in a mixing bowl and stir in the sugar and suet.

2. Beat the eggs and milk together. Mix into the flour briskly with a fork.

3. Stir in the chocolate pieces and spoon the mixture into the basin. Cover with cling film. Pierce the film with the point of a knife.

4. Microwave at full power for 4–4½ minutes, or until the top of the pudding reaches the film.

5. Remove from the oven. Allow to stand for 2 minutes before removing the film.

CLAFOUTIS

Clafoutis

SERVES 4

This is based on a Yorkshire pudding batter and is often made with cherries, which are delicious. Any orchard fruit can be used, but a combination of apples, raisins and cinnamon makes it a cold-weather treat.

Butter for greasing
450g Bramley or Granny Smiths apples, peeled, cored and sliced; keep covered with water containing the juice of half a lemon
50g raisins
1 tablespoon soft brown sugar
1 level teaspoon ground cinnamon
100g plain flour
75g golden caster sugar
3 eggs, beaten
300ml milk
Icing sugar for dusting

1. Preheat the oven to 200°C/gas mark 6.

2. Butter an ovenproof dish and put in the apple slices. Scatter the raisins over the apple. Sprinkle with the brown sugar and cinnamon.

3. In a mixing bowl, sieve the flour and stir in the caster sugar.

4. Beat or whisk in the eggs and then add the milk.

5. Pour the batter over the fruit.

6. Bake for 30–40 minutes in the preheated oven, or until well-risen and golden brown.

7. Dust with icing sugar and serve hot with cream or cold with ice cream.

BREAD-AND-BUTTER PUDDINGS

Here are two of my favourite pudding recipes. The first is a traditional bread-and-butter pudding; the other is my daughter Rebecca's own twist on this recipe.

Bread-and-butter Pudding

SERVES 4

You can use up any stale bread for this recipe.

- Butter for spreading and greasing
- 4 slices white bread, well-buttered, crusts removed if you wish; each slice cut into triangles
- 80g sultanas or raisins or a mix of both
- 3 eggs, beaten
- 280ml milk
- Zest of 1 lemon
- 2 teaspoons vanilla extract
- 50g golden caster sugar
- Grated nutmeg

1. Preheat the oven to 190°C/gas mark 5. Butter an ovenproof dish and arrange the bread in layers, butter-side up.

2. Sprinkle the dried fruit evenly over the bread.

3. Beat the eggs into the milk and stir in the lemon zest and vanilla. Add the sugar and stir again.

4. Pour the egg mixture over the bread and fruit.

5. Top with grated nutmeg to your own taste and leave to stand for 30 minutes. This allows the bread to soak up the custard mixture.

6. Bake for 30–40 minutes in the preheated oven until well-risen and golden brown. For a crispy top to your pudding, sprinkle on a tablespoon of caster sugar before the nutmeg.

7. Serve with cream or custard.

SERVES 4

Chocolate Bread-and-butter Pudding

This uses brioche instead of bread. It gives a richer flavour, but you can still use ordinary bread if you wish.

- Butter for spreading and greasing
- 4 slices brioche, well-buttered and cut into triangles
- 100ml double cream
- 300ml milk
- 100g dark chocolate, broken into small pieces
- 3 eggs, beaten
- 2 tablespoons soft brown sugar
- Grated chocolate for topping

1. Preheat the oven to 190°C /gas mark 5. Butter an ovenproof dish and arrange the brioche evenly over the bottom.

2. In a saucepan, add the cream and the milk, then heat very gently until it feels slightly hotter than your finger. Add the chocolate pieces and allow to melt into the milk. Remove from the heat.

3. Beat in the eggs and stir in the sugar.

4. Pour the milk mixture over the brioche. Allow to stand for 30 minutes.

5. Bake in the preheated oven for 30–40 minutes, or until well-risen and set to the touch.

6. As soon as the pudding is cooked, sprinkle over some grated chocolate; this will melt into the surface.

7. Serve warm with cream.

Cheesecakes

These have to be high on many people's favourite dessert list, so here are three very different recipes for you to try. The easiest way to make the biscuit crumbs is to put the correct amount of biscuits into a plastic food bag, tie it securely and crush them with a rolling pin. Great fun!

Simple Cheesecake

SERVES 6

Butter for greasing
250g digestive biscuits, crushed into coarse crumbs
100g unsalted butter, melted
200g icing sugar
300g tub cream cheese
Juice of 1 lemon
300ml whipping cream

1. Butter a loose-bottomed 22cm round cake tin. Combine the biscuit crumbs and melted butter in a bowl and press down firmly into the tin. Chill in the fridge for 40–45 minutes.

2. Meanwhile, make the filling by creaming the icing sugar, cream cheese and lemon juice in a mixing bowl.

3. In a separate bowl, whip the cream until it forms soft peaks, then fold into the cheese mixture.

4. Pour the filling onto the base immediately and return to the fridge. Leave to set for 1–1½ hours.

Serving suggestion
Top with your favourite fresh fruit, a little extra cream or the chocolate sauce below.

Chocolate Sauce

100g dark chocolate
50ml double cream
1 tablespoon golden syrup

1. Melt the chocolate in a bowl over a pan of hot water.

2. Stir in the cream and syrup.

3. Serve drizzled over cheesecake or ice cream.

SERVES 8–10

Baked Vanilla Cheesecake

This is my personal favourite. It is a very rich, creamy cheesecake that needs very little accompaniment when serving. It is ideal as a special-occasion dessert and tastes better if prepared the day before and allowed to mature for at least 24 hours.

Both this cheesecake and the chocolate cheesecake recipe are easier to lift in and out of the oven if you place the tin on a baking tray.

Butter for greasing
300g digestive biscuits, crushed
120g unsalted butter, melted
200g extra thick double cream
600g soft cream cheese, light or full-fat
½ teaspoon vanilla extract
230g icing sugar
1 egg, beaten

1. Butter a 22cm loose-bottomed tin. Combine the biscuit crumbs and melted butter in a bowl and press down firmly into the base of the tin. Place in the fridge for 30–40 minutes.

2. Preheat the oven to 150°C/gas mark 2. Beat the cream and cheese together in a mixing bowl and add the vanilla, sugar and egg. Mix until smooth.

3. Pour onto the base and cook in the preheated oven for 1 hour 20 minutes. Turn off the oven and leave the cheesecake inside to cool. Remove and refrigerate until time for serving.

Storage
This will keep for 3–4 days in a covered container in the fridge.

Hot-chocolate Cheesecake

SERVES 8

Butter for greasing
200g double chocolate chip cookies, crushed
100g unsalted butter, melted
1 egg
150g golden caster sugar
800g full-fat soft cheese
150g dark chocolate, melted in a bowl over a pan of hot water

1. Butter a 22cm loose-bottomed tin. Mix the biscuit crumbs and melted butter together in a bowl and press into the base of the tin. Place in the fridge for 30–40 minutes.

2. Preheat the oven to 150°C/gas mark 2. Beat the egg and sugar into the cheese and stir in the melted chocolate.

3. Pour the filling over the base and bake for 1 hour 20 minutes. Allow to cool for 20–30 minutes before serving with cream or chocolate sauce.

Cookies with Cappuccino Zabaglione

This is a wonderful dessert to make for a dinner party. You can make the cookies beforehand, even the day before they are to be served, so long as they are kept in an airtight container. Or make the dough and keep it in the fridge or freezer until you are ready to bake them.

For the cookies

150g butter
120g Demerara sugar
120g golden caster sugar
280g plain flour
1 egg
200g chocolate chips, buttons or chopped chocolate
Butter for greasing

For the zabaglione

6 egg yolks (reserve the whites for the meringue recipe on the next page)
3 tablespoons caster sugar
120ml strong black coffee, cool
1 tablespoon Tia Maria, optional
250ml double cream

To make the cookies

1. Cream the butter and sugars together until light and fluffy.

2. Add a tablespoon of flour and beat in the egg.

3. Fold in the rest of the flour and mix in the chocolate. Combine to form a dough.

4. Roll into a log shape and chill for at least an hour. Freeze at this point if necessary.

5. Preheat the oven to 190°C/gas mark 5. Slice the dough into 1cm rounds and place flat-side down on a greased baking sheet, 2cm apart.

6. Bake in the preheated oven for 15–20 minutes.

7. Leave on the tray to cool slightly before transferring to a wire rack.

To make the zabaglione

1. Put the egg yolks and sugar in a bowl over simmering water and whisk together until light and fluffy.

2. Add the coffee and Tia Maria (if using) and continue to whisk until the mixture forms soft peaks.

3. In a separate bowl, whisk the double cream until it forms soft peaks.

4. Remove the egg mixture from the heat and fold the cream into the egg mixture.

5. Spoon into glasses and serve with the cookies.

SERVES 4

Meringue

A meringue is such a versatile dessert base: it can be used to make pavlova, which can hold many different fruits and fillings. Drizzle it with melted chocolate to vary the base, or make into small, individual meringues and serve them as cakes. The meringue itself can also be made into an Eton Mess, where it is broken up and mixed with cream and chopped strawberries or raspberries.

The secret of making successful meringue is to use a grease-free bowl. The way I make sure of this is by wiping half a lemon around the bowl before using it, then wiping it again with kitchen paper. Bake the meringue on silicone paper to ensure that it doesn't stick.

3 egg whites serves about 4 people (you can use the ones left over from the zabaglione recipe for this)
For every egg white, use 55g caster sugar

1. Preheat the oven to 150°C/gas mark 2.

2. Place the egg whites in a clean, grease-free bowl and whisk until they form peaks. This should take about 3–4 minutes.

3. Add the sugar 2 tablespoons at a time and whisk in.

4. When all the sugar is whisked in, the meringue should be glossy and firm.

5. Place a sheet of silicone paper on a baking sheet; a little of the meringue mixture underneath will help the paper stay in place.

6. Using a metal tablespoon, spoon the mixture onto the baking sheet, forming it into a circle about 20cm in diameter. Put more spoonfuls around the edge of the circle to raise the sides if you're making a pavlova.

7. Just before putting the meringue in the oven, turn the heat down to 140°C/gas mark 1. Bake for 1 hour, then turn off the heat, but leave the meringue inside to dry out in the cooling oven.

TRIFLE

There are many ways of making a trifle. Some contain jelly and fruit, others have sponge in them. Here are three of my favourites.

Sherry Trifle

SERVES 6

This is the one I make most often. I use a can of thick cream for the top, but you can use whipping cream whisked enough to thicken but not too stiff. It is much easier to make the custard with custard powder rather than the egg version, as it thickens more readily and still tastes delicious.

6 trifle sponges, or the equivalent amount of homemade sponge cake
300g canned strawberries or raspberries
5 tablespoons pale cream sherry

For the custard
600ml whole milk
2 rounded tablespoons custard powder
1 tablespoon sugar

To finish
1 x 280g or 2 x 170g cans sterilised thick cream
1 chocolate Flake
6–8 glacé cherries

1. Arrange the sponges in the bottom of a trifle bowl. Break them up slightly to fit if necessary.

2. Spoon over the fruit and enough juice to moisten the sponge.

3. Pour in the sherry and leave to soak.

To make the custard
You can also use a 170g can of evaporated milk made up to 600ml with a mixture of milk and water. This makes the custard taste even creamier.

1. In a jug, mix 4 tablespoons of milk with the custard powder and sugar to make a paste. Heat the rest of the milk in a saucepan.

2. When the milk starts to simmer, pour in the custard powder paste, whisking well to get rid of any lumps.

3. Once thickened, pour the custard back into the jug and allow it to cool completely before using in the trifle.

To finish the trifle
1. Spoon the custard over the fruit base.

2. Shake the can of cream, open and smooth it over the custard.

3. Crush the chocolate Flake before opening, then sprinkle over the top of the trifle. Decorate with the glacé cherries.

> *Tip*
> To stop a skin forming on the custard, put a disc of baking or greaseproof paper on the top of it while it cools.

TRIFLE

SERVES 6–8

Black Forest Trifle

This is based on the black forest gateau recipe that was popular back in the 1970s. All the sections of the trifle (except for the cream) may be prepared in advance and put together just before serving.

For the sponge
Butter for greasing
100g butter
100g caster sugar
1 egg
80g self-raising flour
20g cocoa powder

For the chocolate custard
2 tablespoons cornflour
2 tablespoons caster sugar
500ml milk or 1 x 170g can evaporated milk made up to 500ml with milk and water
100g dark chocolate, chopped finely

You will also need
1 x 300g can or jar of black cherries in their own juice
2 tablespoons kirsch, optional
300ml double cream
A little grated chocolate for the top

To make the sponge

1. Preheat the oven to 190°C/gas mark 5. Grease and line a square nonstick baking tin.

2. Cream the butter and sugar together and beat in the egg.

3. Sieve the flour and cocoa powder together into the creamed mixture.

4. Put into the tin and bake for 20–25 minutes, or until well-risen and springy to the touch.

5. Allow to cool completely before using in the trifle.

To make the chocolate custard

1. In a heatproof jug, mix the cornflour and sugar together with 3 tablespoons of the milk and stir until smooth.

2. Heat the rest of the milk in a pan but do not boil.

3. Pour the hot milk into the cornflour mixture, mix well and return to the pan.

4. Bring to the boil, stirring constantly. As soon as boiling point is reached, turn the heat down and simmer for 2 minutes.

5. Remove from the heat and stir in the chocolate. Continue stirring until all the chocolate has melted and the custard looks evenly coloured.

6. Cool completely before using.

To assemble the trifle

1. In a large trifle bowl, arrange the chocolate cake over the bottom and spoon over the cherries and enough of the juice to moisten the sponge. Sprinkle in the kirsch, if using.

2. Spread the custard evenly over the sponge and fruit.

3. Whip the double cream until it forms soft peaks and spread over the custard.

4. Top with the chocolate.

TRIFLE

SERVES 6

Jelly-based Trifle

Use any fruit you wish for this and add a little cake to the jelly while it is still warm. Strawberry jelly and fruit cocktail go well together, or use sliced fresh strawberries in the summer. For an unusual variation, try using a can of tropical fruits and a lime jelly.

- 1 strawberry jelly, made according to the packet instructions, using fruit juice as well as water
- 1 x 300g can fruit cocktail (or fruit of your choice)
- Broken up sponge cake, optional
- 600ml homemade custard (see page 156)
- Either 1 x 280g can thick sterilised cream or 300ml double cream
- Glacé cherries, chocolate flakes or hundreds and thousands

1. Pour the jelly into a trifle bowl and stir in the fruit and cake, if using. Refrigerate until set.

2. Spoon over the custard and spread it evenly over the jelly.

3. If using double cream, whisk until it forms peaks and spread over the custard. If using a can of cream, shake well and spoon over the custard.

4. Decorate as you wish with your favourite topping.

SERVES 6 OR MAKES 6 INDIVIDUAL SERVINGS

Baked Custard Creams

This recipe is very versatile as the creams can be served as they are, or made into crème brûlées or crème caramels. They can also be served with fruit underneath or as a cold dessert with a fruit topping. You can make a large one in a buttered soufflé or deep pie dish or individual ones in buttered ramekins.

2 tablespoons caster sugar
2 eggs
2 egg yolks
½ teaspoon vanilla extract
400ml double cream
Butter for greasing
Grated nutmeg, optional

1. Preheat the oven to 170°C/gas mark 3. Whisk the sugar into the eggs and egg yolks.

2. Stir the vanilla into the cream and heat gently either in a saucepan or the microwave until it is hot, but not boiling. Pour into the egg mixture, whisking gently.

3. Strain the mixture through a fine sieve and pour into a large, lightly buttered soufflé dish or individual buttered ramekins. Sprinkle with a little grated nutmeg if you like.

4. Stand the dishes in a roasting pan with sufficient hot water to come a third of the way up the dishes.

5. Bake in the preheated oven for 1 hour for a single large one, or for 40–50 minutes for individual ones. Serve warm, but allowing it to cool gives a better flavour.

Crème Brûlée

To make this, simply use single cream instead of milk and cream. Then, after baking, preheat the grill and sprinkle the custards with some brown sugar. Place under the hot grill until the sugar caramelises and bubbles. Allow to cool completely before serving.

Crème Caramel

To make the caramel, put 150g golden caster sugar in a pan with 50ml water. Bring to the boil without stirring, until the mixture turns brown and thickens. Before pouring the custard, spoon the caramel into the bottom of the dish(es) and bake as before in the custard recipe, following steps 4 and 5.

ICE CREAM AND SORBETS

Making your own ice creams and sorbets doesn't require an ice-cream maker. Although they are useful, it can be done easily without. And once you have tasted your own ice cream, only the most expensive varieties will be anything like as delicious.

Sorbets can be made with most fruits, and it is a great way to use and preserve any fruit that is in season.

The wonderful thing about making ice creams, ices and sorbets is that, not only do they taste better, but you are in control of the ingredients. They will keep for several months in the freezer, and you can have a selection of everybody's favourite on hand at any one time.

Vanilla Ice Cream

This recipe uses double cream, as it produces a better-textured product than those with less fat content. Fewer crystals form in the freezing process, and this makes preparation easier.

Have a space ready in your freezer for the ice cream. One hour before the mixture is ready for freezing, set your freezer at its coldest setting, because the ice cream will have a better texture if it is frozen quickly. Any ice crystals that form during the process will also be smaller and easier to break up.

4 whole eggs
2 egg yolks
150g caster sugar
300ml double cream
300ml whole milk
1 teaspoon vanilla extract

1. Whisk the eggs, yolks and sugar together.

2. In a large saucepan, heat the cream, milk and vanilla together, whisking gently. When the cream is hot (not boiling), stir in the egg mixture.

3. Transfer the custard back to the pan. Cook the custard, whisking gently and continuously, until the mixture thickens. This will take about 10–12 minutes.

4. Pour into a freezeable container and freeze for 1 hour, then lift out and beat with a wooden spoon.

5. Repeat the beating after the second hour, then leave to freeze for at least 4–5 hours more before serving. This will produce a smoother-textured ice cream, because the beating breaks up any crystals that may form.

Chocolate Ice Cream

80ml water
150g caster sugar
400g dark chocolate, broken into small pieces
3 egg yolks
600ml double cream

1. Put the water and sugar in a saucepan over a low heat, stirring to dissolve the sugar. Bring to the boil, then simmer for 5 minutes.

2. Remove from the heat and add the chocolate pieces. Stir gently until all the chocolate has melted.

3. Beat in the egg yolks.

4. Whisk the cream until thick, but not stiff, and fold it into the chocolate mixture with a metal spoon.

5. Pour into a freezeable container and freeze for 1 hour, then lift out and beat with a wooden spoon.

6. Repeat the beating after the second hour, then leave to freeze for 4–5 hours before serving.

Strawberry Ice Cream

This is the easiest ice cream to make and can be made in the morning to be ready for serving in the afternoon.

500g fresh strawberries, hulled and halved
220g caster sugar
500ml double cream

1. Purée the strawberries with half of the sugar, either by mashing them by hand or preferably in a food processor.

2. Pour the purée into a bowl and whisk in the cream and the rest of the sugar.

3. Put into a lidded, freezeable container and freeze for at least 4 hours, or until firm.

Tutti-frutti Ice Cream

30g raisins
30g sultanas
25g chopped glacé cherries
2 tablespoons Cointreau or brandy
1 quantity vanilla ice cream custard (see page 160)

1. Put the dried fruit in a bowl and sprinkle with the Cointreau or brandy. Leave to soak for 30 minutes, stirring now and again.

2. Make the custard as in the vanilla ice cream recipe (steps 1, 2 and 3).

3. Stir the soaked fruit into the custard and freeze as for vanilla ice cream.

SORBETS

The great thing about sorbets is that they can be made with most fruits. Perfect for a hot summer's day!

Raspberry Sorbet

450g thawed, frozen or fresh raspberries
100g caster sugar
140ml water
1 egg white

1. Mash the raspberries or blend to a purée in a food processor.

2. Push the purée through a sieve into a bowl.

3. In a small saucepan, dissolve the sugar in the water. When it is thoroughly dissolved, bring to the boil for 5 minutes, until thick and syrupy.

4. Mix the syrup into the purée and allow to cool. Then transfer to a freezeable container and freeze for about an hour.

5. Whisk the egg white until stiff, then remove the sorbet from the freezer and fold in the egg white.

6. Put the sorbet back in the freezer and leave until well-frozen.

SORBETS

Lemon Sorbet

Zest and juice of 3 lemons (see step 1)
500ml water
200g caster sugar

1. Take the zest from the lemons by paring away the very top layer of the skin with a small, sharp knife and putting it in a pan with the water and sugar. Heat until the sugar dissolves.

2. Simmer the mixture for 5 minutes, then allow to cool completely. Remove the lemon zest. Chop a small quantity of the zest into very thin strips and add back to the syrup.

3. Add the lemon juice and whisk in.

4. Pour the mixture into a freezeable lidded container and freeze for 30 minutes.

5. Remove from the freezer and whisk the mixture. Do this once more after 30 minutes, then allow to freeze thoroughly.

Variation
For lemon-lime sorbet, simply substitute 1 lime for 1 of the lemons. All other quantities remain the same.

Orange Sorbet

2 oranges
250ml water
200g caster sugar
250ml fresh orange juice

1. Juice the oranges. Reserve some of the flesh (without the pith) if you wish.

2. In a saucepan, heat the water with the sugar and allow the sugar to dissolve fully before boiling for 4–5 minutes.

3. Add the orange juice (and flesh, if using) and allow to cool completely.

4. Put the mixture in a freezeable, lidded container and freeze for 30 minutes before whisking. Repeat this once more, then freeze fully.

SORBETS

Mango Sorbet

4 very ripe mangoes, peeled and cubed (keep all the juice)
Juice of 2 lemons or limes
180g caster sugar
180ml water

1. Purée the mangoes in a food processor, then add the lemon or lime juice.

2. In a saucepan, dissolve the sugar in the water and bring to the boil for 5 minutes until the syrup thickens.

3. Put the mango purée and juice in a bowl and pour in the syrup. Whisk it in and allow it to cool thoroughly before whisking again and pouring it into a freezeable, lidded container.

4. Freeze for 30 minutes, then whisk. Repeat this once more before freezing completely.

PUDDINGS AND DESSERTS

My Notes

11

Making Pickles

When you can create a foodstuff from all kinds of ingredients and make them taste quite different, but at the same time quite similar, you have to be some kind of kitchen wizard. Yet making pickles does just that – and it doesn't require any extraordinary magic at all. I used to love watching my mother get all excited at harvest time, pickling onions and cauliflower, and of course, making that wonderful brown pickle we all now buy from the shops. Mother always said she was preparing for winter, 'Just in case we get snowed in.' And we did, too, in 1963 – but we never once ran out of food.

Pickles are an excellent way of preserving a wide range of foodstuffs, from onions and red cabbage to eggs and cucumbers. They don't contain many ingredients, apart from vinegar and some spices, and are very easy to make. So long as the jar has a good, secure seal they will keep well for a year. A pickle tastes better after it has matured in the vinegar for a few weeks (some recipes say two months).

There are four main types of pickle: cooked, uncooked, sweet vegetable and fruit pickles. When making pickles of any kind, however, DO NOT use pans made of copper: vinegar reacts badly with this metal and spoils the preserve. Any glass jars must have secure lids made of plastic or with a plastic lining; again, this is because the vinegar corrodes metal over time, and eventually the pickles would spoil. Glass jars with snap-down lids, such as Kilner jars, are ideal because any metal is located only on the outside and the lid is glass with a safe rubber seal.

Muslin bags are useful to have if you're using whole spices and don't particularly want them in your finished pickle. A muslin square gathered

SIX STEPS TO PERFECT PICKLES

Step 1: Prepare the Vinegar

Make sure that you use high-quality vinegar, whether malt, brown or the white distilled type. You can use cider and wine vinegars, but their flavour is lost among the full-blown taste of the pickles themselves. When recipes do use these vinegars, they are for delicate-tasting fruit or vegetables. Pickling vinegar is spiced with many different ingredients and tastes best when these are allowed to flavour the vinegar over a period of time. Whole spices are usually used because they infuse gradually. The amount of spices used depends on whether you want a sweet, hot or mild pickle.

For a sweet pickle
1 litre vinegar
280g brown sugar
½ teaspoon salt
4 whole cloves
½ teaspoon mixed allspice berries and white peppercorns
¼ teaspoon ground cinnamon
¼ teaspoon ground ginger

For mild pickles
1 litre vinegar
¼ teaspoon each of cloves, cinnamon bark, mace, allspice berries and white peppercorns

For hot pickles
1 litre vinegar
25g each of allspice and mustard seed
15g each of white peppercorns and whole cloves
½ teaspoon dried crushed chillies

1. For all sweet pickle recipes, pour the vinegar into a jug and dissolve the sugar by stirring constantly until all the granules have disappeared. Check on the back of the spoon that none are sticking.

2. For all types of pickle recipes, pour the vinegar into a storage jar. Put the various spices, either in a muslin bag or loose, into the jar with the vinegar.

3. Leave to mature for 6–8 weeks, shaking the jar gently from time to time to ensure that the flavours blend well.

Quick Spiced Vinegar

If you haven't prepared any vinegar and get a chance to make some pickles, try this:

1. Pour sufficient vinegar to cover your pickles into a double boiler, or use a heatproof glass bowl over a pan of cold water. Add a quantity of ready-mixed pickling spice; the correct quantity should be on the packet.

2. Bring to the boil, then remove from heat but keep the vinegar bowl in the hot water so that both it and the pan cool down together.

3. Strain if you wish and use for your pickles.

SIX STEPS TO PERFECT PICKLES

Step 2: Prepare the Fruit and Vegetables

Peel and wash all items being made into pickles; they must all be of good quality or they will all spoil. Prepare them as each recipe requires. If they are being pickled whole, all items will require pricking all over.

Step 3: Treat with Brine

Vegetables keep and taste better if soaked in brine before pickling. This helps kill off any bacteria that will spoil the look and taste of the finished pickle and cut down the storage life.

120g coarse salt to every litre of water; do not use table salt as this will cloud the finished pickle

Using brine

1. Submerge the fruit or vegetables to be pickled in a brine solution.

Using salt

Some recipes require vegetables to be salted rather than put in brine.

1. Place the vegetable in thin layers in a large dish and salt each layer, finishing with a layer of salt. Don't be afraid to be liberal with the amount, as every part of the vegetables needs covering. This step usually lasts 24 hours.

Step 4: Rinse

After salting, drain the brine or remove the salt and rinse thoroughly in cold water. This is best done in a colander under a running tap because the salt clears much more quickly.

SIX STEPS TO PERFECT PICKLES

Step 5: Bottle

• Large jars are best for pickling. Choose ones that will hold about 1kg of pickles.

• All jars and lids must be sterilised; once again screw-top or snap-on Kilner-type lids are the most secure. A loose lid means loss of liquid through evaporation.

• When bottling, it is best to pour a little of the vinegar into the jar before packing in the vegetables. This ensures that the pickles are completely covered with vinegar and that there are no air pockets at the bottom of the jar.

• Pour the rest of the vinegar over the pickles and cover by at least 2cm.

• Tap the jars to release any air pockets and seal straight away.

If you have any vinegar left over, either slice some onions and/or cucumbers and pour on the leftover vinegar with a little extra salt and pepper. Leave to infuse for an hour and you have an instant accompaniment to meat-and-potato pie or a hotpot.

Step 6: Store

• Most uncooked pickles need to be left in a cool, dark place to mature for at least 2 months, but check the recipes; some, such as red cabbage, are ready for eating after a few days. Cooked pickles are usually ready after a few weeks of maturing; again, check the individual recipes for exact times.

• All pickles should be stored in a dark, cool place, and most will keep well for 6 months if unopened.

Note: All 'Makes x jars' quantities for the following recipes are approximate.

UNCOOKED PICKLE RECIPES

Pickled Onions

MAKES 6–7 x 450G JARS

3kg shallots or pickling onions
1 litre spiced vinegar (see page 168)
Coarse salt for brining

1. Soak the peeled onions in a brine solution (see page 169) for 36 hours; no need to prick them due to their small size.

2. Rinse well and pack into sterile jars.

3. Cover with the vinegar and seal well.

4. Leave for at least 2 months before consuming.

Pickled Red Cabbage

MAKES 4–5 x 450G JARS

1 large red cabbage
About 1 litre spiced vinegar (see page 168)
Coarse salt

1. Shred the cabbage and layer it in a dish, sprinkling each layer liberally with salt (see page 169). Leave for 24 hours.

2. Rinse the cabbage thoroughly and pack into sterile jars, covering with the vinegar. Seal immediately.

3. This is ready to eat after 5 days, but must be consumed within 3 months if unopened.

Variation
White cabbage may be prepared in the same way, but it will keep for just 2 months.

MAKES 4–5 x 450G JARS

Pickled Cauliflower

Pickled cauliflower tastes best if the vinegar is slightly sweet. Add 2 teaspoons of white granulated sugar per 500ml of vinegar a few days before it is needed.

4 cauliflower heads
1 litre spiced vinegar (see page 168)
Sugar, see above

For the brine
300g coarse salt
1 litre water

1. Wash the cauliflower heads well and cut them into small florets.
2. Soak in a brine solution for 24 hours (see page 169).
3. Rinse well and drain. Pat dry with a cloth.
4. Pack into sterile jars and cover with the vinegar. Seal immediately.

Storage
This is best left for 1 month before consuming and will keep for 6 months unopened.

Pickled Cucumbers

MAKES 3 x 450G JARS

3 medium cucumbers
Coarse salt
580ml spiced vinegar (see page 168)

1. Wash and dry the cucumbers and chop into thick slices. Layer the slices in a dish and salt each layer liberally (see page 169). Leave for 24 hours.
2. Just before it's needed, heat the spiced vinegar so that it is barely simmering.
3. Drain the cucumber liquid and rinse off the salt. Pack the cucumber into sterile jars and cover with the hot vinegar. Seal well immediately. This will be ready to eat after 5 days.

Storage
This will keep for up to 6 months unopened.

UNCOOKED PICKLE RECIPES

MAKES 2 x 450G JARS

Pickled Walnuts

When collecting walnuts for pickling, do so at the end of June or beginning of July, while the nuts are still young. Always wear gloves both for picking and pricking the walnuts: the juice that comes out of them is dark brown and stains fingers. It is very difficult to remove, so beware!

1kg walnuts
580ml spiced vinegar (see page 168), sweetened with 2 teaspoons of granulated sugar)

For the brine
300g coarse salt
1 litre water

1. Prick the walnuts with a large pin or needle and soak in a brine solution for 48 hours (see page 169).

2. Drain and soak for a second time in a fresh brine solution for 5 more days.

3. Drain and leave exposed to the air for 24 hours, or until the walnuts turn black.

4. Pack them into sterile jars and cover with the sweet spiced vinegar. Seal immediately. These are ready for eating in about 5–6 weeks.

Pickled Gherkins

MAKES 2–3 x 450G JARS

Gherkins are very small cucumbers and are my favourite pickle.

1kg gherkins
580ml spiced vinegar (see page 168)

For the brine
300g coarse salt
1 litre water

1. Wash the gherkins and prick all over before soaking in brine for 3 days (see page 169).

2. Drain and rinse in hot water.

3. Heat the vinegar in a large pan and bring to the boil.

4. Add the gherkins and remove from the heat.

5. Allow the pickles to cool for 1 hour before bottling and sealing well.

Storage
Leave the gherkins for at least a month before eating. They should keep for 6–9 months unopened.

MAKES 6–7 x 450G JARS

Onion, Cauliflower and Cucumber Pickle

1kg each pickling onions, cucumbers and cauliflower
Coarse salt
1 litre spiced vinegar (see page 168)
A few dried chillies

1. Prepare the vegetables by peeling the onions, slicing the cucumber and breaking the cauliflower into small florets.

2. Layer the vegetables in a large dish and pour salt over each layer (see page 169). Leave for 24 hours.

3. Rinse off the salt and dry well. Pack into sterile jars, adding a chilli now and again.

4. Cover with the vinegar and seal immediately. This is ready to eat in about 8 weeks.

COOKED PICKLE RECIPES

MAKES 4 x 450G JARS

Brown Pickle

This recipe is pretty near the ploughman's pickle we all love, but whose name I am not going to mention because they wouldn't like me telling everyone that you can make it a lot cheaper than you can buy it!

It is fairly easy to prepare and really does have that tang. You can replace some of the ingredients depending on what you have available, but the dates, apples and sugar are really quite important.

- 250g carrots, peeled and chopped into 5mm cubes
- 1 medium swede, peeled and chopped into 5mm cubes
- 4–5 garlic cloves, peeled and finely chopped or grated
- 125g dates, very finely chopped
- 2 onions, peeled and finely chopped
- 2 medium apples, chopped into 5mm cubes
- 15 small gherkins, chopped into 5mm cubes
- 250g dark-brown sugar
- 1 teaspoon salt
- 4 tablespoons lemon juice
- 500ml malt vinegar
- 2 teaspoons mustard seeds
- 2 teaspoons ground allspice

1. Combine all the ingredients in a large pan and bring them to the boil slowly, making sure that everything is completely mixed.

2. When the pickle is boiling, reduce the heat so that it is just simmering and keep this temperature for around 2 hours, stirring every few minutes or so to make sure the bottom of the pan doesn't catch and the pickle remains well mixed. You can add a little water if the mixture is becoming too stiff.

3. When the vegetables are just becoming soft, spoon the pickle into sterile jars.

4. Leave for about 5–7 days before eating.

MAKES 4 x 450G JARS

Piccalilli

This is the North of England's historic pickle, where, particularly in Yorkshire, it is traditional to serve with bacon and eggs and more or less everything! There are plenty of variations, but real piccalilli has plenty of cauliflower in it.

1.5kg vegetables (cauliflower sprigs, baby onions, cucumbers or gherkins)
600ml white vinegar
100g sugar
15g dry English mustard
15g ground ginger
10g turmeric
1 level tablespoon cornflour

For the brine
300g salt
1 litre cold water

1. Clean all the vegetables and peel those you want to peel. Chop them finely or coarsely, depending on your preference.

2. Make the brine by dissolving the salt in the litre of water. Soak the vegetables for 24 hours. Drain and dry them.

3. Put all the vinegar except 2 tablespoons with the sugar, mustard and spices into a large saucepan and heat gently until the sugar has dissolved.

4. Add the vegetables and simmer gently until they are crisp but have a softness about them.

5. Make a paste with the cornflour and the 2 tablespoons of vinegar and stir it into the pickle. Bring the liquid to a strong boil, stirring all the time. Simmer for about 3 minutes, then remove from the heat.

6. Bottle in sterile containers. The longer you can leave this pickle, the better it will taste. Leave for at least 7 days.

Pickled Beetroot

MAKES 5–6 x 450G JARS

2kg beetroot
1.5 litres spiced vinegar (see page 168)

1. Scrub the beetroot without damaging the skins. Wrap in foil and bake in the oven for 1½ hours at 180°C/gas mark 4 until tender.

2. Wearing rubber gloves, peel any thick parts of the beetroot skin away and cut the beetroot into thick slices.

3. Pack into sterile jars and cover with the vinegar; the sweetened version may be used if you prefer. Leave for 4 days before consuming.

Storage
This pickle has a shelf life of 2 months.

COOKED PICKLE RECIPES

MAKES 3 x 450G JARS

Vegetable Marrow Pickle

1.5kg marrow, cubed
2 level teaspoons salt
1 teaspoon each
of ground ginger,
mustard powder,
salt and turmeric
5 whole cloves
225g white sugar
1 litre vinegar

1. Sprinkle the marrow with the salt and leave overnight.

2. Strain and rinse thoroughly.

3. Put all the other ingredients in a saucepan and bring to the boil. Cook at boiling for 10 minutes.

4. Add the marrow and reduce to simmering. Cook for 30–40 minutes, or until tender.

5. Cool for 5 minutes, stir and pour into sterile jars. Seal immediately.

Red Tomato Pickle

MAKES 4 x 450G JARS

This is really for those who grow their own tomatoes and have loads to contend with at one time. If you wish, make half the quantity.

3kg ripe red tomatoes
1 litre spiced vinegar
(see page 168)

1. If the tomatoes are small, leave them whole. Otherwise, cut in half.

2. Place in an ovenproof dish and pour over sufficient vinegar to cover. Cover and cook in the oven for about 30–40 minutes at180°C/gas mark 4.

3. Put the tomatoes in sterile jars and cover with the hot vinegar. Seal immediately. Let them mature for 4 weeks before serving.

Variation
Add 4 tablespoons of sugar to the vinegar before pouring over the tomatoes.

FRUIT PICKLES

Making pickle is an interesting way to preserve a glut of fruit. They can be served with cold meats and cheeses, eaten as a dessert with cream or used in a winter fruit salad.

Apple Pickle

MAKES 3–4 x 450G JARS

580ml sweet spiced vinegar (see page 168)
1kg sugar
1kg cooking apples

1. Put the vinegar in the pan and stir in the sugar, stirring occasionally. Heat to dissolve the sugar.

2. Meanwhile, prepare the apples by peeling, coring and chopping them. Put them into the pan with the vinegar immediately so that they don't turn brown.

3. Bring to the boil and cook until the apples are tender. Lift out the fruit and put into sterile jars.

4. Boil the vinegar syrup until it has reduced by half.

5. Pour over the fruit and seal immediately. Leave to mature for 3 weeks before use.

Crab-apple Pickle

MAKES 3–4 x 450G JARS

Use plain malt vinegar for this recipe.

580ml malt vinegar
Piece of cinnamon stick
5 cloves
5 black peppercorns
1.5kg crab apples
2 tablespoons lemon juice
1kg sugar

1. Put the vinegar and spices into a saucepan. Bring to the boil, then cook at simmering for 10 minutes.

2. Leave to cool for 1 hour, then remove the spices.

3. Wash the apples and remove the stalks. Cook in another pan with the lemon juice and just enough water to cover until the apples are tender.

4. Measure 280ml of the apple juice from the pan and add to the vinegar. (Discard the rest of the juice.)

5. Stir in the sugar and heat until dissolved.

6. Add the apples, bring to the boil and cook for 10 minutes. Lift the fruit out of the vinegar and put into prepared sterilised jars.

7. Boil the rest of the vinegar syrup until it has reduced by half, then pour over the fruit. Seal immediately. Leave for 4 weeks before eating.

Pickled Plums

MAKES 3–4 x 450G JARS

For this recipe use firm, medium-sized fruit, either just ripe or nearly ripe. Any of the paler plums, such as Victoria, work best in this recipe.

1kg just-ripe plums
580ml sweet spiced white vinegar (see page 168)
Juice of 1 lemon
1kg sugar

1. Wash the plums and prick them all over.

2. Put the vinegar, lemon juice and sugar in a saucepan, bring to a boil, and boil for 5 minutes. Add the plums and simmer until tender.

3. Remove the plums and put into sterile jars. Reduce the vinegar syrup by half then pour over the plums. Seal immediately.

4. Allow to mature for 8–10 weeks before using.

MAKES 1 x 2-LITRE JAR

Pickled Eggs

You will need a wide-necked, 2-litre screw-top or Kilner-type jar for this recipe. It uses wine vinegar rather than malt because eggs need a milder flavour.

- 12 free-range, very fresh eggs
- 25g ready-made pickling spice
- 8 whole cloves
- 1.2 litres white-wine vinegar

1. Hard-boil the eggs and leave them to cool completely in very cold water.

2. Put the spices in a muslin bag and put this and the vinegar in a saucepan. Bring to the boil and simmer for 10 minutes. Leave to cool before removing the spice bag.

3. Put some of the cooled vinegar in a sterile jar, filling it about a quarter of the way up.

4. Shell the eggs and put them in the jar. Fill the jar with the vinegar and seal it immediately. The eggs will be ready to eat in 5–6 weeks.

What might go wrong?

• Very little can go wrong with this incredibly easy way of preserving. So long as you adhere to the steps of preparation, there should be very few problems.

• One problem that can occur in pickles which have been stored for a long time is cloudy vinegar. If there is a small amount of sediment floating about, it is simply bits from the pickles themselves and is nothing to worry about. But if the whole jar is cloudy, this is probably due either to poor-quality vinegar, using too little salt or treating the ingredients for too short a period during the brining or salting stage. Any completely cloudy jars should be discarded.

• With a cooked pickle, the only real problem is shrinkage. This is due to a poor seal on the lid, which allows the liquid in the pickle to evaporate, so always make sure the lids are airtight when sealing.

MAKING PICKLES

My Notes

Strawberry
Mandarins in
Syrup
Marmalade
Blackcurrant
Conserve

12

Jams and Other Preserves

When I first started making jam, it was because we had too much fruit. We used as much as we could, but we still had loads of 'leftovers', so Paul made a batch of funny-tasting wine out of all of them put together. It was such a disaster that I decided I would make jam the next year, and I have never looked back.

Making jam and preserves of all kinds is much easier and quicker than you think – you no longer have to spend hours over a hot pan. You don't need to make jars and jars of the same kind, either, as all the recipes in this chapter make between three and five 450g jars.

TIPS AND TECHNIQUES

Jam-making Essentials

Besides fruit and sugar, there are two essential ingredients that make jam- and preserve-making successful, and they work together to produce a set preserve. The first is pectin, a gel-like substance found in varying degrees in most fruit, usually in the skin, pips and membranes. Combined with fruit acid and sugar, pectin makes a good setting agent. Some fruit contains little pectin, however, so it must be added during cooking. You can usually buy it in granular form in 13g sachets. The same applies to fruit acid: extra can be added by using lemon juice.

Equipment
You don't need lots of new equipment; just have the following to hand:

- A large, sturdy-based pan. A maslin pan suitable for all preserve-making costs around £35.
- A long-handled spoon (I use a wooden one)
- A ladle
- Some sterilised jars with good-fitting lids; screw-tops or Kilner-type jars are ideal. It's best to have an extra jar around just in case you need it, as quantities can never be precise.
- Sticky labels – to remind you what is in the jar and when it was made
- A jam funnel: the only thing I advise buying specially. It makes filling the jars much easier.
- A jam-making thermometer: this indicates when jam has reached setting point, so it can be useful, but you'll still need to test for setting to be sure.

Choosing the produce
When making any preserves, choose the freshest, ripest, most perfect fruit and vegetables you can. This will guarantee that your preserve will remain fresh and uncontaminated. Successful jam may be made with frozen fruit so long as it is fully defrosted before using. You can make jam with any kind of sugar, but white granulated sugar does the job and is probably the most economical.

Working with sugar
Heat the sugar in a roasting pan in the oven for 10 minutes on a very low temperature. This helps the sugar dissolve more quickly in the fruit. To check whether sugar has dissolved, simply look at the mixture on the back of the spoon; if it looks grainy, it hasn't.

Testing for setting point
Place a saucer in the fridge to test the jam on after boiling. Put a very small amount of jam on your cold plate, allow it to cool, then push it gently with your finger. It should wrinkle and stay in place if setting point is reached. Don't worry if it moves a little; so long as it wrinkles and doesn't run round your finger, it is ready to pot.

JAMS

Strawberry Jam

1kg strawberries, washed and hulled
Juice of 1 lemon
1 x 13g sachet pectin
1kg white granulated sugar

1. Put the strawberries in a large pan on a medium heat. Use a masher to squash down some of the fruit, but leave some whole to add texture to the finished jam. Add the lemon juice.

2. Bring the fruit to a fast simmer and cook for 2–3 minutes, or until some of the strawberries are soft. Lower the heat slightly.

3. Sprinkle in the pectin and sugar and stir until all the sugar is dissolved. Bring to the boil and cook at boiling point for 4 minutes.

4. Remove from the heat and test for setting with the cold saucer. If it isn't ready, boil for 30 seconds more and repeat the test. As soon as setting point is reached, remove from the heat, stir and leave to cool for 5 minutes.

5. Stir to distribute the fruit before ladling it into pots. Seal the pots immediately and label when cool.

Storage
This will keep for up to 1 year unopened.

Raspberry Jam

1kg raspberries, washed and hulled
Juice of 1 lemon
1kg granulated sugar

1. Put the fruit in a large pan and simmer for 8–10 minutes, or until the juice runs freely and the fruit has softened.

2. Remove from the heat and stir in the lemon juice.

3. Place the pan back on a medium heat, add the sugar and stir until it has dissolved. Bring to the boil and cook at boiling for 4–5 minutes.

4. Remove from the heat and test for setting. When setting point is reached, leave to cool for 5 minutes.

5. Stir to distribute the fruit, then ladle into prepared jars and seal immediately. Label when cool.

Storage
This will keep for up to 1 year unopened.

Blackcurrant Jam

1kg blackcurrants, washed, topped and tailed
500ml water
1.5kg sugar

1. Put the fruit and water in the pan and bring to the boil. Reduce the heat and simmer for 25–30 minutes, or until the fruit is tender. Stir occasionally.

2. Remove from heat, stir in the sugar and keep stirring until it has all dissolved.

3. Bring to the boil and continue boiling for 5 minutes, stirring from time to time.

4. Test for setting point. When it has been reached, allow the jam to cool for 5 minutes, then stir and ladle it into prepared jars. Label when cool.

Storage
This will keep for up to 1 year unopened.

Blackberry and Apple Jam

About 500g Bramley apples, peeled, cored and chopped
130ml water
1kg blackberries, washed and hulled
Juice of 1 lemon
1.5kg sugar

1. Simmer the apples with the water for 10 minutes, or until they begin to soften.

2. Add the blackberries and lemon juice and simmer until the apples are completely soft and the blackberries are tender.

3. Add the sugar and stir on a low heat until it is completely dissolved.

4. Boil rapidly for 8–10 minutes, then test for setting point.

5. Cool for 5 minutes, stir and ladle it into prepared jars. Label when cool.

Storage
This will keep for up to 1 year unopened.

Plum Jam

Using the freshest English plums ensures the fruit has the highest quantity of pectin, so you don't have to add any more.

1.5kg Victoria or other English plums, stoned and halved
280ml water
1.5kg sugar

1. If you don't want large pieces of fruit in the jam, cut the plums into chunks.
2. Place the fruit in a pan with the water and simmer until the liquid has reduced by half. This will take about 15–20 minutes.
3. Add the sugar and stir until it has dissolved completely.
4. Bring to the boil and cook at boiling for 6–8 minutes.
5. Test for setting point. Once reached, leave for 5 minutes to cool, stir, then ladle the jam into prepared jars. Label when cool.

Storage
This will keep for up to 1 year unopened.

Gooseberry Jam

1.5kg gooseberries, topped and tailed
430ml water
2kg sugar

1. In a large saucepan, simmer the gooseberries with the water for about 20 minutes, until the berries start popping their skins.
2. Add the sugar and stir on a low heat until it has completely dissolved.
3. Turn up the heat and boil for 10 minutes, then test for setting point.
4. Once setting point has been reached, allow the jam to cool for 5 minutes, stir, then ladle it into prepared jars. Label when cool.

Storage
This will keep for up to 1 year unopened.

Summer Fruit Jam

This is made with 1kg of frozen summer fruits, but it can also be made with the same quantity of any mixed frozen fruit, or simply raspberries or strawberries. Pectin needs to be added because fruit starts to lose its natural pectin content once frozen.

2 x 500g packs of frozen summer fruits, defrosted
1kg sugar
1 x 13g sachet pectin

1. Place the fruit in the saucepan over a low heat and simmer for 2 minutes.

2. Add the sugar and pectin and stir until it has completely dissolved.

3. Bring to the boil and cook at boiling for 4 minutes, then test for setting.

4. Once setting point has been reached, allow the jam to cool for 5 minutes before stirring and ladling it into prepared jars. Label when cool.

Storage
This will keep for up to 1 year unopened.

MARMALADE

All the following marmalade recipes will keep for up to 1 year unopened.

Seville Orange Marmalade

Because the season for this fruit is very short in this country, it is best to make more than a few jars of this at one time – it has to be said it is the best-tasting marmalade, after all! This recipe makes about 6 x 450g jars.

900g Seville oranges
1 lemon
2 litres water
1.5kg sugar

1. Wash the oranges and lemon, then juice them into a jug. Retain all pips, peel and bits of flesh.

2. Put the water in a pan along with the lemon peel and pour in the orange and lemon juice.

3. Cut all the orange peel into very thin strips – don't discard anything. Put the pips and any large bits of pith into a square of muslin; tie up the muslin square securely and place it in the pan. Add any bits of flesh to the water.

4. Put the shreds of peel into the water and bring to the boil, then reduce the heat slightly so that it is still simmering very fast and cook for 2 hours.

5. When the peel is tender and the pith has mostly dissolved into the liquid, remove the muslin bag with clean tongs and place onto a plate to cool.

6. Turn down the heat and add the sugar. Stir until completely dissolved. Squeeze the muslin bag over the pan and stir. Discard the bag.

7. Bring the marmalade mixture to the boil and continue to boil for 15 minutes.

8. Test for setting point using a cold saucer, if a drop wrinkles when pushed, it is ready for potting. Allow to cool for 5 minutes in the pan, then stir and ladle into prepared jars. Label when cool.

Old English Marmalade

This is the traditional dark-brown marmalade that tastes so good in puddings. It is made in exactly the same way as the marmalade on page 189.

900g Seville oranges
1 lemon
2 litres water
1 dessertspoon dark treacle
500g white granulated sugar
1kg brown sugar

Follow the recipe as before, but add the treacle before you stir in the two sugars. Make sure the brown sugar is completely dissolved, as it takes longer than the white sugar.

Microwave Orange Marmalade

So quick and easy, this recipe makes 1 large or 2 small jars, so it is ideal if that's all you want.

3 small, juicy oranges
500g sugar
1 lemon
500ml water

1. Cut the oranges in half and juice them, reserving the peels. Pour the juice in a large bowl that will just fit into your microwave: it must be big enough to contain the marmalade when it rises during boiling. Do the same with the lemon.

2. Put the pips in a muslin square, tie the muslin securely and put into the juice.

3. Put the lemon peels in the juice and cut up the orange peel as finely as you wish. Put in the bowl. Boil 300ml of the water and pour over the peel and juice.

4. Microwave on high for 15–20 minutes, or until the peel is tender.

5. Remove the muslin bag and lemon peels with tongs, squeezing out as much of the juice as possible.

6. Stir in the sugar and keep stirring until it is all dissolved.

7. Add 200ml of boiling water, put back in the microwave and cook on high for 20 minutes. Stop and stir the mixture at least 3 times during cooking.

8. Leave to cool for 5 minutes, then stir and ladle into prepared jars.

MAKES ABOUT 3 X 450G JARS

Lemon Marmalade

6 lemons
900ml water
800g sugar

1. Scrub the lemons and peel off the rind, leaving as much pith on the fruit as possible.

2. Cut the rind as thinly as possible and put in a large saucepan. Pour in the water.

3. Juice the lemons and put the juice in the pan.

4. Cut up the rest of the fruit and put any large pieces of pith and the pips in a muslin square. Add to the pan.

5. Bring the lemon and water mixture to the boil then simmer until the peel is tender; this will take about 1½–2 hours.

6. Remove the muslin bag and squeeze out all the juice; use tongs or two spoons to do this.

7. Stir in the sugar and bring to the boil. Boil for 15 minutes.

8. Test for setting. Allow to cool for 5 minutes before stirring, then ladle the marmalade into prepared jars. Label when cool.

Variations

• To make lemon-lime marmalade, simply use 3 lemons and 3 limes in the recipe.

• For lime marmalade, use 4 limes instead of the lemons and follow the recipe as before.

MAKES ABOUT 3 X 450G JARS

Lemon Curd

This isn't really a 'preserve' because it doesn't keep for much longer than 4 weeks unopened, and 7 days if opened and kept in the fridge. But it is easy to make and delicious in cakes and tarts.

4 lemons
225g butter
450g caster sugar
5 eggs

1. Finely grate the peel of the lemons and squeeze out the juice. Put both in a bowl over a pan of simmering water.

2. Add the butter and sugar and stir gently until the sugar has dissolved.

3. In a separate bowl, beat the eggs. Remove the pan from heat and add the eggs to the bowl gradually, beating in well.

4. Return the pan to a low heat and stir the contents in the bowl until the mixture becomes like thick cream.

5. Pot immediately into prepared jars and seal well. Label when cool.

MAKES ABOUT 5 X 450G JARS

Peach and Brandy Conserve

This is a delicious treat and makes an excellent gift.

1.5kg ripe peaches
150ml water
Zest and juice of 1 lemon
100g flaked almonds
80g glacé cherries, halved
1 x 13g sachet pectin
1kg sugar
5 tablespoons brandy

1. Cut up the peaches and remove the stones. Remove the skins as well if you wish.

2. Place the peach pieces in a saucepan and add the water, lemon zest and juice and simmer for 5 minutes.

3. Add the almonds and cherries and simmer for another 5 minutes, or until the peaches are just tender.

4. Stir in the pectin and sugar. When the sugar has completely dissolved, bring to the boil and boil for 4 minutes.

5. Remove from the heat and test for setting point. If it is ready, stir in the brandy. Leave for 5 minutes to cool.

6. Stir well and pour into prepared jars. Label when cool.

Storage
This will keep for a year unopened.

MAKES ABOUT 5 X 450G JARS

Easy Mincemeat

This is very quick and easy to make. You'll wonder why you never made your own mincemeat before!

450g cooking apples, cored and diced
225g vegetarian suet
280g soft brown sugar
1kg mixed dried fruit: raisins, sultanas and currants
110g glacé cherries, halved
½ teaspoon mixed spice
½ teaspoon cinnamon
½ teaspoon grated nutmeg
Juice and zest of 1 lemon
5 tablespoons brandy

1. Stew the apples on a low heat until tender. Leave to cool.

2. Meanwhile, mix all the other ingredients together in a big bowl, making sure everything is well-coated in the brandy.

3. When the apples are cool, mix them into the other ingredients, making sure everything is thoroughly combined.

4. Pack into prepared jars and seal well.

Serving and storage
This tastes at its best when left to mature for 2 weeks. It will keep for 4–5 months in a cool, dark place.

CHUTNEY

These are also easy to make and taste much better than shop-bought chutney.

Tomato Chutney

MAKES ABOUT 4 X 450G JARS

The ideal accompaniment to burgers and hot dogs.

1.5kg ripe tomatoes, chopped
1 medium onion, finely chopped
200ml malt vinegar
1 teaspoon mixed spice
½ teaspoon paprika
½ teaspoon cayenne pepper
1 garlic clove, chopped finely
1 level dessertspoon salt
200g soft brown sugar

1. Put all the ingredients except the sugar into a large pan and heat to simmering. Simmer for 5 minutes.

2. Add the sugar and stir until it has all dissolved.

3. Cook for 45–50 minutes until the mixture has thickened.

4. Ladle into prepared jars and seal immediately. Label when cool.

Serving and storage
Leave to mature for 2 weeks before consuming. Once opened, store in the fridge.

Mango Chutney

MAKES 2–3 X 450G JARS

3 underripe mangoes, peeled and diced
2 teaspoons salt
4 garlic cloves, chopped
350ml white vinegar
350g soft brown sugar
4 tablespoons sultanas
½ teaspoon turmeric
1 level teaspoon salt

1. Put the mangoes in a dish and cover with the 2 teaspoons of salt. Leave overnight.

2. Rinse and dry the mangoes and put them in a large pan with all the other ingredients. Heat slowly until all the sugar has dissolved, and then boil rapidly for 2–3 minutes. Turn down the heat and simmer for 45–50 minutes, or until the mixture is thick.

3. Stir and allow to cool for 5 minutes. Ladle into prepared jars and seal immediately. Cool before labelling. Mature for at least 7 days before consuming.

MAKES 1 SMALL JAR

Quick Red Onion Chutney

This may be consumed as soon as it is cool. Double the amounts if you want to make more than a single jar.

- 2 large or 3 small red onions, peeled and chopped finely
- 1 red pepper, chopped into small pieces
- 5 tablespoons brown sugar
- 100ml white-wine vinegar
- ½ teaspoon salt
- 1 garlic clove, chopped

1. Put all the ingredients into a pan and heat gently, stirring until all the sugar has dissolved.

2. Bring to the boil, then turn down the heat and simmer for 40–45 minutes until thick and glossy.

3. Stir and ladle immediately into the prepared jar. Leave to cool before serving.

JAM AND OTHER PRESERVES

My Notes

13

Cakes, Biscuits and Slices

If someone asked me the question 'What do you like to cook the most?', my answer would be the title of this chapter. There is an endless supply of recipes from a very few ingredients, and if you have the basics in your fridge and cupboards, you can create the most wonderful cakes and biscuits whenever you feel the urge. Don't worry if you're not very successful with a recipe at first; it won't matter because everything will be edible so long as nothing is too burned! Just have a go and enjoy the experience of creating your own delicious homemade cakes and biscuits.

Baking Essentials

A very basic stock of baking ingredients should contain:

- Plain and self-raising flours
- Eggs
- Golden caster, icing and soft brown sugars
- Cocoa powder
- Golden syrup
- Oats
- Dried fruit, mixes or single varieties like raisins, sultanas and currants
- Baking powder
- Butter. I have baked with other fats, but butter generally produces the best flavour and texture.
- Jam
- Vanilla extract

There are other ingredients used in the recipes in this chapter, of course, but these are the basics.

Utensils

Good baking tins and sheets are an essential part of successful baking. If you want to make a variety of cakes and biscuits; a basic set should include:

- 2 x 18cm or 20cm round sandwich tins
- 1 x 20cm round loose-bottomed (springform) cake tin. The loose bottom helps with removal of the cake after baking.
- 1 loaf tin
- 1 shallow rectangular tray-type tin measuring about 30cm down the longest side
- 2 baking sheets. I find enamelled metal the best and most hard-wearing.
- 1 or 2 x 12-hole bun tins
- 1 x 12-hole muffin tin

You should also have on hand a large mixing bowl, a wooden spoon, a silicone or plastic spatula for scraping all the mixture out of the bowl and a large metal spoon or tablespoon.

TIPS AND TECHNIQUES

Techniques for cake preparation

Creaming is the process of combining butter, sugar and air to produce a light-textured cake, and it is the most frequently used technique. To do it effectively, always make sure the butter is at room temperature. Use either a wooden or silicone spoon to combine the butter and sugar. Beat the butter until soft, then add the sugar. Continue to beat the butter and sugar together until the mixture becomes lighter in colour and fluffy in texture. This can be done with a hand mixer to speed up the process, but don't overbeat; otherwise the air will start to escape and have the opposite effect.

Rubbing in is the method most commonly used in making shortbreads and some fruit loaves. The flour is sifted into a mixing bowl and the butter is added in small pieces, rubbed into the flour using the fingertips. Air is incorporated by raising the mixture as high as sensible as it is rubbed in. The mixture should resemble breadcrumbs.

Folding in is the process of combining flour and the creamed mixture in a way that retains as much air in the cake as possible. Sifted flour is gradually added to creamed butter and sugar. Using a large metal spoon, cut into the mixture in one sweeping action, turning it over to combine. Mix the flour into the butter-sugar cream this way until it has all been incorporated.

Dropping consistency is when a cake mixture is moist enough to fall readily off the spoon without any shaking. It means the mixture is ready to bake.

Tips for successful cake-making

- Preheat the oven to the correct temperature.
- Read the recipe all the way through and prepare and weigh all the ingredients before you begin.
- Measure all ingredients accurately.
- Prepare any required tins or baking sheets before you start.
- Times given for cooking are approximate and will depend on your oven, so always bear this in mind when baking your own cakes.
- When a cake is baked, transfer it to a cooling tray or wire rack. This allows air to circulate around the cake, cooling it more quickly and evenly.

MAKES AT LEAST 10 LARGE SLICES

Victoria Sandwich

This is a very traditional cake, but one my family and I never get bored with. It uses a simple creaming-in method that may easily be adapted for other recipes. Although this recipe uses jam as a filling, you could also try using lemon curd, marmalade or cooked or fresh fruit.

200g butter, at room temperature
200g golden caster sugar
200g self-raising flour
3 eggs, beaten
2–3 tablespoons milk
Approximately 4 tablespoons of your favourite jam for filling

1. Preheat the oven to 170°C/gas mark 3. Grease 2 x 20cm round sandwich tins and line them with baking parchment.

2. Cream the butter and sugar together in a mixing bowl until lighter in colour and fluffy in texture.

3. Add a tablespoon of the flour and gradually beat in the eggs. Using a metal tablespoon, fold in the rest of the flour.

4. Stir in the milk and divide the mixture evenly between the tins.

5. Level out the tops of each cake and make a shallow well in the centre. Bake for 18–20 minutes, or until risen and golden. Test to see if the sponge is cooked by pressing it with your finger; it should feel springy and bounce back to shape. If not, bake for a few more minutes and repeat the test.

6. Remove from the oven and allow to cool for 15 minutes before lifting the cakes, still wrapped in the baking parchment, out of the tin. Cool for 5 more minutes before peeling off the parchment.

7. When the cakes are completely cool, spread the top of one with the jam or other filling and sandwich together.

8. Put on a serving plate. I use an upturned tin lid lined with a paper doily; then you can more easily cover the cake with the tin. Dust a little caster sugar on the top before serving. Will keep for 5–6 days in an airtight tin.

Variation

You can also use this mixture to make fairy cakes, butterfly cakes and jam buns. See the next page to learn how!

MAKES AT LEAST 24 SMALL BUNS OR 15 MUFFIN-SIZED CAKES

Fairy Cakes

I quantity of Victoria Sandwich cake mix (previous page)

For the glacé icing
100g icing sugar
Sufficient water to mix to a thick but spreadable topping
Topping of your choice

1. Preheat the oven to 170°C/gas mark 3.

2. Line two 12-hole tartlet or muffin tins with fairy-cake cases. Follow the Victoria Sandwich instructions, pour the batter into the cases and bake for 12–15 minutes until springy to the touch and golden brown.

3. To make the icing, sieve the icing sugar into a bowl and mix with 2 tablespoons of water. Add more water, a teaspoon at a time, until the icing is thick enough to stay on top of the cakes.

4. Allow the cakes to cool completely before icing the top of each. Top with cherries, chocolate buttons, hundreds and thousands or anything that looks fun and tasty. These will keep for 4–5 days in an airtight tin.

Butterfly Cakes

Fairy cakes, as above

For the butter cream
80g butter
120g icing sugar

1. Make fairy cakes as above and allow to cool.

2. To make the butter cream, cream the butter until light and fluffy, then sift in the icing sugar and beat until smooth and light.

3. Cut a circle out of the centre of each cake and put a teaspoon of the butter cream in the space. Cut the top in half and place the halves back in the centre of the butter cream to form 'butterfly wings'.

4. Dust with icing sugar. These will keep for 2–3 days in an airtight tin.

Jam Buns

I quantity unbaked Fairy Cakes
Your favourite jam
Icing sugar for dusting

1. Make the fairy cakes mixture as above, but before baking, drop half a teaspoon of your favourite jam into the centre of each cake. As they bake, the jam will drop to the bottom of the sponge.

2. When cooked and cooled, dust them with icing sugar. These will keep for 5–6 days in an airtight tin.

Chocolate Sandwich Cake

150g butter
150g golden caster sugar
140g self-raising flour
2 eggs, beaten
25g cocoa powder
4 tablespoons milk

For the filling
50g dark chocolate
50g butter
80g icing sugar

1. Preheat the oven to 170°C/gas mark 3. Grease 2 x 18cm round cake tins and line them with baking parchment.

2. To make the sponge, cream the butter and sugar together until light and fluffy.

3. Add a tablespoon of the flour, then beat in the eggs gradually.

4. Sift the rest of the flour and cocoa powder together and fold into the creamed mixture.

5. Stir in the milk and divide the mixture between the two tins.

6. Smooth over the top and make a well in the centre of each cake to ensure even cooking.

7. Bake for 18–20 minutes, then test to see if the sponge is cooked by pressing it with your finger; it should feel springy and bounce back to shape. If not, bake for a few more minutes and repeat the test.

8. Remove from the oven and allow to cool for 15 minutes before lifting the cakes, still wrapped in the baking parchment, out of the tin. Cool for 5 more minutes before peeling off the parchment.

To make the filling

1. Melt the chocolate in a bain-marie or a heatproof bowl placed over a pan of hot water.

2. Cream the butter until soft and sift in the icing sugar. Cream in the sugar and stir in the melted chocolate.

3. Spread the filling over the top of one cake and sandwich the two cakes together.

4. Put the cake on a serving plate or on an upturned tin lid and dust with a combination of cocoa powder and icing sugar. This will keep for 3–4 days in an airtight tin.

Vanilla Sandwich Cake

When I was a child, this was called a Russian sandwich cake. It has a vanilla custard filling, but the actual name for this kind of custard is confectioner's custard or *crème pâtissière.*

For the sponge
150g butter
150g golden caster sugar
150g self-raising flour
2 eggs
½ teaspoon vanilla extract
4 tablespoons milk

For the custard filling
3 egg yolks
65g golden caster sugar
20g cornflour
250ml milk
½ teaspoon vanilla extract

1. Preheat the oven to 170°C/gas mark 3. Grease 2 x 20cm round sandwich tins and line them with baking parchment.

2. Cream the butter and sugar together in a mixing bowl until lighter in colour and fluffy in texture.

3. Add a tablespoon of the flour and gradually beat in the eggs and vanilla. Using a metal tablespoon, fold in the rest of the flour.

4. Stir in the milk and divide the mixture evenly between the tins.

5. Level out the tops of each cake and make a shallow well in the centre. Bake for 18–20 minutes, or until risen and golden. Test to see if the sponge is cooked by pressing it with your finger; it should feel springy and bounce back to shape. If not, bake for a few more minutes and repeat the test.

6. Remove from the oven and allow to cool for 15 minutes before lifting the cakes, still wrapped in the baking parchment, out of the tin. Cool for 5 more minutes before peeling off the parchment.

7. To make the custard, beat the egg yolks and sugar together in a bowl until well combined. Add the cornflour and mix well.

8. Heat the milk in a pan until hot, but not boiling. Pour it slowly over the egg mixture, whisking all the time. Add the vanilla extract and mix well.

9. Return the custard to the pan and heat to boiling point, very gently stirring all the time. Reduce the heat and simmer for 3 minutes, or until thick and smooth. Allow to cool thoroughly.

10. Fill the cake with the vanilla custard and top with some glacé icing (see page 203). This type of cake would traditionally be sprinkled with toasted coconut around the perimeter on top of the icing.

Storage
Cover and store in the fridge. This is best eaten within 48 hours.

Coffee Cake

150g butter
150g soft brown sugar
2 teaspoons good granulated coffee, mixed with a tablespoon of hot water
150g self-raising flour
2 eggs, beaten
2–3 tablespoons milk
2–3 coffee beans to decorate

For the coffee butter cream
75g butter
100g icing sugar
1 teaspoon granulated coffee mixed with 2 teaspoons hot water

1. Preheat the oven to 170°C/gas mark 3. Grease and line a 20cm round loose-bottomed cake tin with baking parchment or greaseproof paper.

2. Cream the butter and sugar together until light and fluffy. Beat in the coffee.

3. Add a tablespoon of the flour and beat in the eggs.

4. Fold in the rest of the flour and stir in sufficient milk to give the batter a dropping consistency.

5. Spoon into the prepared tin and bake for about 35 minutes, or until well-risen and springy to the touch.

6. Allow to cool for 15 minutes in the tin, then remove the tin and transfer to a wire rack to cool completely. Leave for a few minutes before removing the paper.

7. To make the butter cream, beat the butter until soft and cream in the icing sugar and coffee. When the mixture is light and fluffy, it is ready to use.

8. Make sure the cake is completely cold before topping with the butter cream or it will melt. Decorate the finished cake with some grated coffee beans.

Variations
This coffee cake recipe can be varied to make a coffee and walnut or pecan cake. Simply fold 25g chopped walnuts or pecans into the creamed mixture before folding in the flour. Decorate the finished cake with some extra nuts, either left whole or chopped.

Storage
These cakes will keep for 3–4 days in an airtight container.

Crunchy Topped Apple Cake

For the fruit layer
2 Bramley apples, cored peeled and diced
2 tablespoons honey
1 teaspoon cinnamon

For the cake
150g butter
150g golden caster sugar
1 egg, beaten
50ml milk
190g self-raising flour

For the topping
40g butter
2 tablespoons soft brown sugar
80g rolled oats

Tip
For a slice-able cake, make sure the apples are cold before cooking. If you want more of a pudding-like consistency, use warm apples to put on the cake, but put on the topping immediately and bake as quickly as you can, or the cake base will melt.

1. Preheat the oven to 170°C/gas mark 3. Grease and line a loaf tin, measuring approximately 23cm down the long side.

First, make the fruit layer
This needs to be made first and allowed to go completely cool before using.

2. Place the fruit and honey in a saucepan and cook over a low heat until the apples begin to break down or 'fall' (no water needed over a low heat).

3. Add the cinnamon, stir to mix and place in a dish to cool.

Next, make the cake
4. Cream the butter and the sugar together.

5. Beat in the egg and milk and fold in the flour.

6. Spoon the mixture into the prepared tin.

7. When the apple and honey mixture is cool, spread it over the cake mixture.

Finally, make the topping
8. Melt the butter in a pan with the sugar over a very low heat. Remove from the heat and stir in the oats.

9. Spread this over the apple layer and bake for 55–60 minutes. Test to see if the cake is cooked by inserting a skewer into the centre; if the cake is done, the skewer will come out clean. If it isn't done, put the cake back in the oven and bake for 5 more minutes.

10. Cool the cake in the tin for 20 minutes before transferring to a cooling tray or wire rack. Remove the paper after about 5 minutes. This will keep for 4–5 days in an airtight container.

Variations
• Stew 100g of prepared gooseberries with 3 tablespoons honey until soft and allow to cool before using like the apples.

• Stew 120g chopped rhubarb and 3–4 tablespoons honey until soft, cool and use in the same way as the apples.

Lemon Drizzle Loaf

This cake can be made by the all-in-one method, which means every ingredient goes straight into the mixing bowl together – just make sure the flour is sifted into the bowl. You will need to use a hand mixer to get the best results.

150g butter
150g golden caster sugar
170g self-raising flour, sifted
2 eggs, beaten
Juice and zest of 1 lemon

For the icing
60g icing sugar
1-2 tablespoons lemon juice

Very thin strips of lemon zest, not the pith, sufficient to decorate the top of the cake

1. Preheat the oven to 180°C/gas mark 4. Grease a 23cm loaf tin and line it with baking parchment.

2. Put all the ingredients for the cake into a large mixing bowl and whisk together with a hand mixer. Start on the slowest speed, then build up to the fastest as the ingredients begin to be incorporated. Whisk for about 5 minutes, or until the mixture is lighter in colour.

3. Spoon into the prepared tin and bake for 30–40 minutes. The cake should be a deep golden colour and springy to the touch.

4. Cool in the tin for 15 minutes, then transfer to a cooling tray or wire rack. Remove the paper after 5 minutes.

5. Make the icing by sifting the icing sugar into a small bowl, then mixing in the lemon juice a tablespoon at a time until the icing is fairly runny.

6. Put the cake onto a serving plate and drizzle it with the icing. It should fall down the sides of the cake and onto the plate. Sprinkle with some strips of lemon zest.

Variations
If you wish you can split the cake carefully in half with a serrated knife and fill with 3 tablespoons of lemon curd before icing.

Storage
This cake will keep for 4–5 days in an airtight container.

Madeira Cake

This is a very useful cake because it is plain – which means it makes a good base for many different things. It can be sliced and spread with jam, honey or marmalade, or served with stewed or fresh fruit and used as a base for other recipes, like Queen of Puddings and trifles.

150g butter
150g golden caster sugar
180g self-raising flour
4 eggs
Grated zest of 1 lemon

1. Preheat the oven to 180°C/gas mark 4. Grease and line a 20cm round, loose-bottomed cake tin with baking paper.

2. Cream the butter and sugar together in a mixing bowl.

3. Add a tablespoon of the flour and gradually beat in the eggs.

4. Fold in the rest of the flour and lemon zest.

5. Spoon into the prepared tin and bake for about 45–50 minutes. The cake should be golden brown and springy to the touch when done.

6. Cool for 15 minutes in the tin, then transfer to a cooling tray or wire rack and remove the paper after 5 minutes.

Storage
This cake will keep for 6–7 days in an airtight container.

CAKES

Easy Fruit Cake

If you have been worried about making a fruit cake because you think it is difficult, try this recipe. You don't even need a mixing bowl!

350g mixed dried fruit
110g butter
110g soft brown sugar
120ml water
1 level teaspoon mixed spice
1 egg
220g self-raising flour

1. Preheat the oven to 160°C/gas mark 2–3. Grease and line a 20cm round loose-bottomed tin with baking parchment.

2. Place the fruit, butter, sugar, water and spice into a large saucepan and set it over a low heat. Stir gently until the sugar has dissolved into the mixture.

3. Turn up the heat so that the mixture simmers and cook for 15 minutes. Remove from the heat and allow to cool completely.

4. Beat in the egg and stir in the flour.

5. Spoon the mixture into the prepared tin, smooth out the top and bake for 1¼–1½ hours. Test to see if the cake is done by inserting a skewer into the centre; if it comes out clean, it is cooked. If not, bake for 10 more minutes and try again.

6. Leave to cool in the tin for 30 minutes, then transfer to a cooling tray or wire rack and remove the paper when cool.

Storage
This will keep for 2–3 weeks in an airtight tin.

Cherry and Almond Cake

200g butter
200g golden caster sugar
230g self-raising flour
3 eggs
¼ teaspoon
almond essence
120g ground almonds
120g glacé cherries, halved

1. Preheat the oven to 170°C/gas mark 3. Grease a 20cm round loose-bottomed cake tin and line it with baking parchment.

2. Cream the butter and sugar together.

3. Add a tablespoon of the flour and beat in the eggs and almond essence. Stir in the cherries.

4. Sift in the rest of the flour and ground almonds and fold into the mixture.

5. Spoon the mixture into the prepared tin and smooth out the top.

6. Bake for 1½ hours, or until well-risen and golden in colour.

7. Cool in the tin for 20 minutes before transferring to a cooling tray or wire rack. Remove the paper after 5 minutes.

Storage
This will keep for 6–7 days in an airtight tin.

Easy Carrot Cake

- 200ml sunflower or vegetable oil
- 200g golden caster sugar
- 3 eggs, beaten
- 350g grated carrots
- 3 tablespoons raisins or sultanas
- 150g self-raising flour
- 150g self-raising wholemeal flour
- 2 level teaspoons mixed spice
- 2 tablespoons fresh orange juice

For the cream cheese frosting

- 120g cream cheese
- 120g crème fraîche
- 200g icing sugar
- Grated zest of 1 orange

1. Preheat the oven to 180°C/gas mark 4. Grease a 20cm square cake tin and line it with parchment paper.

2. Whisk the oil, sugar and eggs together in a mixing bowl until light and creamy. Stir in the carrots and the fruit.

3. Sieve the flours and spice together but stir in any bits of wholemeal flour that may remain in the sieve. Fold in the combined flours and stir in the orange juice.

4. Pour into the prepared tin and bake for 40–50 minutes. Insert a skewer in the centre to see if it is cooked; if it comes out clean, it's done. If not, then bake for 5 more minutes and try again.

5. Cool in the tin for 10 minutes, then transfer to a cooling tray or wire rack.

6. When cool, either dust with icing sugar or top with the creamy frosting below.

To make the cream cheese frosting

1. Whisk the frosting ingredients together in a bowl. If it is too stiff, add a teaspoon of hot water.

2. Spread evenly over the carrot cake and cut the cake into squares. Sprinkle with a little grated orange zest.

Storage

This cake will keep for 2–3 days if kept in a container in the fridge.

Orange Polenta Cake

This is a change from a flour-based cake and is very moist and tangy. Polenta is simply cornmeal and it is very popular in Italian cookery.

175g butter
175g golden caster sugar
150g ground almonds
2 large eggs
½ teaspoon baking powder
100g polenta
Juice and zest of 1 orange

For the syrup

3 tablespoons honey
Juice and zest of 2 oranges
1 tablespoon brandy or Cointreau, optional

1. Preheat the oven to 180°C/gas mark 4. Grease a 20cm square cake tin and line it with baking parchment.

2. Cream the butter and sugar together in a mixing bowl until light and fluffy. Stir in the almonds and beat in the eggs.

3. Add the baking powder to the polenta and combine well.

4. Mix the polenta into the creamed mixture and add the orange juice and zest.

5. Spoon the mixture into the prepared tin and bake for 20 minutes in the preheated oven, then turn down the heat to 170°C/gas mark 3 and bake for a further 35–40 minutes, or until the cake is firm.

6. Leave the cake in the tin to cool while you make the syrup.

7. In a small pan on a very low heat, stir the honey into the juice and zest of the orange and add the brandy or Cointreau.

8. Prick the cake all over with a skewer and pour the warm juice evenly over the entire cake. Cool for 30 minutes, then remove the cake from the tin and allow it to cool completely before removing the paper.

Serving suggestion

This may be served like a cake or with thin slices of fresh orange and some crème fraîche as a dessert.

MAKES 15 MUFFINS

Chocolate and Courgette Muffins

280g self-raising flour
3 tablespoons cocoa powder
150g soft brown sugar
50g raisins
1 beaten egg
90ml sunflower oil
½ teaspoon vanilla extract
90ml milk
300g grated courgette

1. Preheat the oven to 190°C/gas mark 5. Put some muffin-sized paper cases into a muffin tin.

2. Sift the flour and cocoa powder together into a mixing bowl. Stir in the sugar and the raisins.

3. In a separate bowl, whisk the egg, oil and vanilla together.

4. Fold the egg mixture into the flour and stir in the milk and courgettes.

5. Spoon the mixture into the muffin cases and bake for 20–25 minutes, or until springy to the touch.

Serving suggestion
These go well topped with cream cheese frosting (see page 212).

MAKES 14 FINGERS

Shortbread

This is one of the easiest of all biscuits to make. There is no rolling or cutting; just press the mixture into the tin, bake it and slice it.

100g self-raising flour
100g plain flour
130g softened butter
100g golden caster sugar

There are two methods of making shortbread. Both are very successful, so have a go at both and see which way you prefer.

Preheat the oven to 180°C/gas mark 4. Grease a shallow 18cm x 27cm rectangular tin.

The rubbing in method

1. Sift the flours into a mixing bowl. Cut the butter into small pieces and add to the flour. Rub the butter into the flour until the mixture is fine and looks like breadcrumbs.

2. Sprinkle in the sugar and stir well.

3. Bring the mixture together and knead lightly until a smooth dough is formed.

4. Press the dough down into the tin so that it is evenly distributed. Prick all over with a fork, leaving a 2cm edge.

5. Bake for 25–30 minutes, or until golden brown.

6. Leave in the tin to cool. Cut into 14 finger-sized pieces while the shortbread is still warm.

7. Lift out when completely cool and store in an airtight tin. They will keep fresh for 6–7 days.

The creaming method

1. Cream the butter and sugar together in a mixing bowl until light and fluffy.

2. Sift the flours together into the creamed mixture and mix in with a wooden spoon.

3. Use your hands to bring the mixture to a ball and knead it lightly until it forms a smooth ball.

4. Follow steps 5–8 in the previous method.

MAKES 16–18 SLICES

Flapjacks

This is the easiest biscuit to prepare – and the speediest.

150g butter, plus extra for greasing
150g golden caster sugar
2 tablespoons golden syrup
330g porridge oats

1. Preheat the oven to 170°C/gas mark 3. Butter an 18cm x 27cm rectangular tin.

2. In a large pan, melt the butter, sugar and syrup together.

3. Stir in the oats with a wooden spoon until fully combined with the butter mixture.

4. Press the mixture down evenly into the prepared pan.

5. Bake for 20–25 minutes.

6. Cut into slices while still warm and allow to cool completely in the tin.

Variation
Especially good for around Bonfire Night: replace 1 of the tablespoons of syrup with 1 tablespoon of treacle.

Storage
This keeps for 5–6 days in an airtight tin.

MAKES ABOUT 16 SQUARES

Strawberry Oat Slice

We eat this as a quick breakfast if we're on the go. It is delicious way to use up a glut of strawberries – or just make it when strawberries are cheap.

400g strawberries, washed, hulled and halved
120g golden caster sugar
300g porridge oats
100g butter

1. Preheat the oven to 200°C/gas mark 6. Grease an 18cm x 27cm rectangular tin.

2. Mash the strawberries and sugar together in a mixing bowl. Stir in the oats and mix well.

3. Melt the butter in a saucepan and pour over the oat-and-strawberry mixture. Combine well with a wooden spoon and press into the prepared tin.

4. Bake for 25 minutes.

5. Cut into 16 squares and leave to cool in the tin. When cold, pop in the fridge for 30 minutes before removing from the tin.

Variation
Use raspberries instead of strawberries.

Storage
This will keep for 3–4 days in an airtight tin.

MAKES 20–24

Ginger Biscuits

These taste wonderful – ideal for ginger-lovers!

110g butter
110g golden caster sugar
1 level teaspoon ground ginger
2cm piece of crystallised ginger, chopped very finely
80g plain flour
30g self-raising

1. Preheat the oven to 160°C/gas mark 2–3.

2. Cream the butter and sugar together until light and soft.

3. Add both forms of ginger. Sift in the flours.

4. Mix together with a metal spoon. The dough should be fairly stiff.

5. Bring the dough together with your hands. Break off small pieces and roll each into a ball. Place on a baking sheet – no need to grease – about 2cm apart.

6. Bake for 35–40 minutes, or until they are golden and have spread out.

7. Cool on the sheet for 20 minutes before transferring to a cooling tray or wire rack.

Storage
Store in an airtight tin. They should stay fresh for up to a week.

MAKES ABOUT 25

Cinnamon and Pecan Biscuits

125g butter
110g golden caster sugar
1 egg, beaten
10g plain flour
50g self-raising flour
2 level teaspoons cinnamon
1 tablespoon cocoa powder
50g chopped pecans
Whole pecan for each biscuit, or half will do
Icing sugar for dusting

1. Preheat the oven to 180°C/gas mark 4. Grease 2 baking trays.

2. Cream the butter and sugar together until light and soft. Add the egg and beat in well.

3. Sieve together the flours, cinnamon and cocoa powder.

4. Add the chopped pecans, then a little of the flour mixture and fold into the creamed mixture. Continue folding in the flour until it is all incorporated.

5. Bring the mixture together with your hands, break off small pieces and roll into balls. Lightly press them down onto the baking sheet. Place a whole or half of a pecan into the centre of each biscuit.

6. Bake for 10–12 minutes.

7. After a few minutes' cooling on the baking sheet, transfer to a cooling tray or wire rack.

8. Dust with a little icing sugar before serving.

Storage
These will keep for 5–7 days in an airtight tin.

MAKES ABOUT 20 BISCUITS

Wholewheat Biscuits

These are more like digestive biscuits, and they are great if you want a biscuit that isn't too sweet. They are also good to serve with cheese.

130g softened butter
100g golden caster sugar
1 whole egg and
1 egg yolk
150g wholewheat flour
75g plain white flour

1. Preheat the oven to 180°C/gas mark 4. Grease two baking sheets.

2. Cream the butter and sugar together and beat in the eggs. The mixture should be light and soft.

3. Sieve the two flours together and add to the creamed mixture, folding in gradually.

4. When all the flour is incorporated, bring the mixture together to form a dough.

5. Roll out the dough on a clean, lightly floured surface, cut into rounds and place on the prepared baking sheets.

6. Bake for 10–15 minutes and allow to cool on the baking sheet for a few minutes before transferring to a wire rack.

MAKES 15–20

Melting Moments

I used to make these as a child when I went to stay with my aunt. They really do melt in your mouth.

100g softened butter
80g golden caster sugar
1 egg, beaten
4–5 drops vanilla extract
150g self-raising flour
75g rolled oats
Glacé cherries, halved

1. Preheat the oven to 180°C/gas mark 4. Grease a baking sheet.

2. Cream the butter and sugar together until light and fluffy.

3. Beat in the egg and vanilla.

4. Fold in the flour and bring the mixture together with your hands.

5. Roll small pieces of the dough into balls and roll each in the oats.

6. Place onto the baking sheet and press down to form a round. Space the biscuits about 2cm apart to allow them to spread during baking.

7. Place half a glacé cherry on top of each biscuit and bake for 10–15 minutes.

8. Leave on the baking sheet to cool for 15 minutes before transferring them to a wire rack.

Storage
They will keep for 4–5 days in an airtight container – but they probably won't last that long!

MAKES 12

Chocolate Brownies

180g self-raising flour
20g cocoa powder
100g butter
200g soft brown sugar
1 large egg, beaten
50g real chocolate chips

1. Preheat the oven to 180°C/gas mark 4. Butter an 18cm x 27cm rectangular tin.

2. Sift the flour and cocoa powder into a mixing bowl.

3. Melt the butter and sugar together in a saucepan over a low heat, then pour into the flour mixture. Beat well.

4. Stir in the egg and chocolate chips. Mix thoroughly to form a soft, moist dough.

5. Press down into the tin and bake in the preheated oven for 15–20 minutes. It is difficult to tell if brownies are cooked just by looking, so press the centre of one with your finger; it should give but still remain flat if it's done.

6. Leave to cool in the tin for 20 minutes, then cut into 12 even pieces.

7. Remove from the tin and transfer to a wire rack.

Variations
Add 50g of chopped walnuts or pecans with the chocolate chips if you like them nutty.

Storage
They will keep for 4–5 days in an airtight tin.

MAKES 15–18

Crispy Jumbles

These are great for children to make – with a little help, of course!

100g softened butter
150g soft brown sugar
1 beaten egg
150g self-raising flour
100g dark chocolate, broken into small pieces (or dark chocolate chips)
50g crisped rice cereal

1. Preheat the oven to 180°C/gas mark 4. Grease a baking sheet.

2. Cream the butter and sugar together in a mixing bowl and beat in the egg.

3. Fold in the flour, chocolate and cereal.

4. Put spoonfuls of mixture onto the baking sheet about 3cm apart and bake for 10–15 minutes.

5. Leave to cool for 15 minutes on the baking sheet, then transfer to a wire rack.

Storage
These will keep for 3–4 days in an airtight tin.

MAKES 14–16 FINGERS

Muesli Slice

I use the cheapest muesli for this rather than the luxury heavily fruited variety.

200g butter
200g soft brown sugar
1 teaspoon mixed spice
2 tablespoons honey
350g muesli

1. Preheat the oven to 170°C/gas mark 3. Grease an 18cm x 27cm rectangular tin.

2. Put the butter, sugar, spice and honey together in a saucepan and melt over a low heat. Stir to combine and dissolve the sugar.

3. Remove from the heat and stir in the muesli. Combine the mixture well so that all the muesli is coated in the butter mixture.

4. Spoon into the tin, press down evenly and bake in the preheated oven for 20–25 minutes.

5. Cut into slices while still very hot and leave in the tin to cool completely. Remove and place in a storage tin.

Storage
They will keep for 4–5 days in an airtight tin.

MAKES ABOUT 25

Jam Drops

80g butter
80g golden caster sugar
½ teaspoon
vanilla extract
2 tablespoons milk
150g self-raising flour
30g custard powder
Raspberry jam

1. Preheat the oven to 180°C/gas mark 4. Grease two baking sheets.

2. Cream the butter, sugar and vanilla extract together until light and creamy. Add the milk and beat in.

3. Sift the flour and custard powder together and fold into the creamed mixture gradually. Mix lightly with your hands to form a soft dough.

4. Roll pieces of the dough into balls about the size of a golf ball and place on the baking sheet. Use the end of a wooden spoon to make an indentation in the centre of each.

5. Spoon a little jam into each indentation and bake for 15–20 minutes.

6. Transfer to a wire rack to cool.

Storage
These will keep for 5–6 days in an airtight tin.

MAKES12–14

Oat Crunchy Cookies

120g butter
120g soft brown sugar
3 tablespoons
  golden syrup
160g self-raising flour
150g porridge oats

1. Preheat the oven to 180°C/gas mark 4. Grease 2 baking sheets.

2. Put the butter, sugar and syrup in a pan and heat until the butter has melted.

3. Remove from the heat. Sift in the flour and stir in the oats.

4. Mix everything together well with a wooden spoon.

5. Form a dough with your hands and break off small pieces to roll into golf ball-sized rounds. Press each down onto a baking sheet.

6. Bake for 10–15 minutes.

7. Transfer to a wire rack to cool.

Storage
These will keep for 5–6 days in an airtight tin.

Luxury Caramel Shortbread

You won't need a huge slice of this to feel satisfied. It is a rich-tasting shortbread, filled with caramel and topped with chocolate.

For the shortbread
80g butter
50g golden caster sugar
130g plain flour

For the caramel
397g can condensed milk
50g soft brown sugar
50g butter

For the chocolate
150g dark chocolate
30ml double cream

For the shortbread

1. Preheat the oven to 180°C/gas mark 4. Grease an 18cm x 27cm rectangular tin.

2. Cream the butter and sugar together.

3. Sift in the flour and fold in.

4. Knead together with your hands and combine to form a dough.

5. Bake for 20 minutes in the preheated oven until a light golden-brown.

6. Leave to cool in the tin.

For the caramel

1. Gently heat all three ingredients together in a saucepan over a very low heat. Stir continuously.

2. When the butter has melted, raise the temperature slightly to dissolve the sugar into the mixture.

3. Bring to the boil, then simmer for 5 minutes, or until it thickens and the bubbles get smaller.

4. Pour the hot caramel carefully over the shortbread and leave to go cool.

For the chocolate

1. Break the chocolate into a bowl and add the double cream.

2. Put the bowl over a pan filled with hot water and melt the chocolate. Stir now and then, but not all the time as the chocolate will go grainy.

3. When melted, pour over the caramel.

4. Cool and put in the fridge to firm up.

5. Cut into small rectangles to serve.

My Notes

14
Celebration Family Meals

One Christmas, in far-off student days, our gang of friends decided to make Christmas dinner. Paul cooked the turkey in his digs, another did a pudding, another cooked the trimmings and so on. Then, in a succession of cars, we all brought our various offerings to the feast. While it sounded like a good idea, we ended up spending hours making that dinner, and when we finally got together we were all so tired that none of us enjoyed it!

Don't lose heart, however: we've all learned a lot about cooking since then! Nothing is more satisfying and enjoyable than making a wonderful meal on special occasions for your family and friends. Which is why in this chapter, I've included some ideas for easy yet special family meals that won't involve the cook missing all the fun.

Salad Niçoise

SERVES 6

1 iceberg or cos lettuce, sliced coarsely
18 black olives, pitted
12 cherry tomatoes, halved
10 anchovy fillets, either in oil or salted
50g French green beans blanched in boiling water, or steamed for 4 minutes if you like them softer
3 eggs, boiled for 5 minutes, shelled and quartered

For the dressing
3 tablespoons red-wine vinegar
2 tablespoons extra-virgin olive oil
A little black pepper
½ teaspoon wholegrain mustard
½ teaspoon garlic salt

1. Arrange the lettuce in 6 small bowls and add the olives and tomatoes.

2. If using anchovies in oil, drain them well and chop in half. Arrange them over the salad.

3. Halve the beans and add them to the dish. Finish with the egg.

4. Mix all the dressing ingredients together in a jug and serve with the salads.

Mushroom Pâté

SERVES 6

Knob of butter
6 shallots, peeled and chopped
400g closed-cup mushrooms, chopped
1 garlic clove, grated
100g light soft cheese
Pinch of salt and black pepper

1. Heat the butter in a frying pan and fry the shallots gently. Add the mushrooms and garlic and cook until most of the liquid has evaporated.

2. Put the mushroom mixture in a food processor with the other ingredients. Process until smooth.

3. Spoon into small ramekins and serve with very thin toasted bread triangles.

SERVES 6

Seafood Pancakes

These small, thin pancakes can be made earlier in the day and kept fresh between greaseproof paper and stored in the fridge.

For the pancakes
1 egg
250ml milk
Black pepper to taste
½ teaspoon dried parsley
80g plain flour
A pinch of salt
Oil for frying

For the filling
4 tablespoons crème fraîche
1 tablespoon double cream
2 tablespoons mayonnaise
1 tablespoon tomato purée
Salt and black pepper to taste
50g mussels, shelled
200g prawns, cooked and peeled

For the pancakes

1. Whisk the egg into the milk. Add the black pepper and the parsley.

2. Sift the flour and salt together into a bowl and gradually whisk in the egg and milk mixture.

3. Add a tiny amount of oil to a small pancake pan and ladle about 2 tablespoons of mixture into the pan. Fry for 2 minutes, then turn over and fry for 20–30 seconds. Repeat until you have sufficient pancakes for your starter.

4. Keep on a plate separated by greaseproof paper until needed. Any leftover mixture may be stored in the fridge for up to 2 days. Stir before use.

For the filling

1. Combine the first 5 ingredients in a bowl.

2. Stir in the mussels and prawns.

3. Put a small spoonful of the filling into a pancake, then roll it up and secure with a cocktail stick if necessary. Repeat until all the pancakes are filled.

Serving suggestion
Serve with rocket leaves and a slice of lemon or homemade mayonnaise.

STARTERS

SERVES 6

Avocado and Mozzarella Salad

2 large beef tomatoes, each sliced into 6 thin slices
2 ripe avocados, peeled and cut into thin slices
150g mozzarella cheese, cut into 12 slices
2 spring onions, chopped very finely

For the dressing
3 tablespoons white-wine vinegar
2 tablespoons olive oil
1 tablespoon runny honey
1 tablespoon chopped chives
Salt and pepper to taste

1. Mix all the ingredients for the dressing together and whisk to combine.

2. Arrange the tomatoes, avocado and mozzarella alternately on small plates.

3. Sprinkle the spring onions over the salad and pour the dressing over it.

MAIN COURSE DISHES

SERVES 6

4 medium carrots, peeled and cut into batons or thick strips
1 small turnip, peeled and cubed
200g French green beans, topped and tailed
25g butter
Salt and pepper to taste

1. Steam or boil the carrots and turnip together for 4 minutes, then add the beans and cook for a further 4 minutes.

2. Place in a casserole dish and add the butter. Mix the vegetables with the butter until they are coated and season to taste.

3. Serve with the venison pie on the next page.

SERVES 6

Venison Pie

This is a really rich-tasting pie, and everything may be prepared well ahead to give you more time with your guests. It is wonderful served with mustard mashed potato and glazed vegetables.

- Half a quantity of shortcrust pastry (see page 90)
- 1 large onion, sliced
- Oil for frying
- 350g venison stewing meat, cut into cubes
- 250g lean stewing beef, cubed
- 2 rounded tablespoons plain flour, sifted together with ½ teaspoon salt, a little black pepper and ½ teaspoon of mustard powder
- 250ml beef stock (see page 17)
- 120ml red wine
- 1 tablespoon tomato purée
- 1 teaspoon thyme
- 100g closed-cup mushrooms, halved

1. Make the pastry and leave it to rest in the fridge. This can be done the day before and wrapped in cling film.

2. Fry the onion in a little oil until soft.

3. Toss the meat in the seasoned flour, covering well, and dust off the excess.

4. Fry the meat with the onions for a few minutes until brown and transfer to a lidded casserole. Add a little of the stock to the frying pan to loosen the juices and pour over the meat.

5. Add the rest of the stock, the wine, tomato purée and thyme and stir well. Season with a little extra salt and black pepper and cover with the lid.

6. Cook for 1 hour at 170°C/gas mark 3. Remove from the oven and stir in the mushrooms. Cook for a further 40 minutes.

7. Pour the meat into a deep pie dish. Allow to cool while you roll out the pastry. It is better to allow the meat to go cool before putting on the pastry, as it allows the flavours of the meat to develop.

8. Roll out the pastry to fit the dish and lay it on top of the meat.

9. Bake at 190°C/gas mark 5 for 25 minutes, or until the pastry is golden. Serve hot.

SERVES 6

Devilled Shoulder of Lamb with Minted Garden Peas

If you can get fresh peas, it is always worth the effort of podding them, but frozen are almost as good these days.

1.5–2kg shoulder of lamb
30g flour seasoned with ¼ teaspoon salt and a pinch of black pepper

For the crust
2 tablespoons Dijon mustard
1 teaspoon paprika
½ teaspoon cayenne pepper
Pinch of white pepper
½ teaspoon salt
25g butter
1 tablespoon lemon juice

For the peas
250g shelled garden peas (about 800g–1kg unshelled) or use the same amount of frozen
About 14 mint leaves
25g butter

1. Place the lamb in a roasting pan and pour 2cm of water around the meat. This keeps it juicy during cooking.

2. Rub the flour into the fat and cook the meat for 40 minutes at 190°C/gas mark 5.

3. Mix all the crust ingredients together. Remove the meat from the oven and cut slits into the fat. Rub the crust into the fat – use the back of a large spoon – and into the slits.

4. Cook for a further 40–50 minutes. Allow it to rest for 20 minutes before carving.

5. Use the juices to make a little gravy. Pour any liquid and juices into a small saucepan and scrape off any tasty debris from the bottom of the pan; use a little hot water to help you. Bring to the boil.

6. Mix a teaspoon of flour or gravy powder with 4 teaspoons of water and pour into the hot sauce; stir until the gravy boils. Serve with the meat in a gravy boat.

7. Serve with the minted garden peas and buttered new potatoes.

For the peas
1. Cook the peas until tender in a little boiling salted water.

2. Chop the mint leaves until very fine and mix with the butter.

3. Drain the peas and place in a serving dish. Add the butter and stir gently to coat the peas.

SERVES 6

Pork in Cider

- 1 medium onion, chopped finely
- Butter for frying
- 1 Bramley apple, peeled and sliced
- 6 pork steaks
- 200ml cider
- 3 handfuls spinach
- 150ml double cream
- Salt and black pepper to taste

1. Preheat the oven to 180°C/gas mark 4.

2. Fry the onions in a little butter until soft. Add the apple slices and cook for 2–3 minutes. Put the mixture into an ovenproof dish.

3. In the same pan, fry the steaks lightly on both sides and place on top of the onions and apples.

4. Pour in the cider and cover the dish.

5. Place in the oven and cook for 25 minutes in the preheated oven.

6. Remove from the oven and stir in the spinach and cream. Season to taste.

7. Heat for 10 minutes in the oven before serving.

Serving suggestion

This is good served with steamed cauliflower and Dauphinoise potatoes (see page 134).

Slow-cooked Beef Curry with Cucumber Raita

This is easy to prepare and can be cooking long before your guests arrive. It isn't too spicy, so most people will enjoy the rich-tasting, melt-in-your-mouth meat.

30g butter
2 large onions, sliced
1 red pepper, sliced
1 green pepper, sliced
1kg lean stewing beef, cut into chunks
1 teaspoon ground cumin
1 teaspoon ground coriander
1 teaspoon turmeric
1 teaspoon mild madras powder
½ teaspoon dried thyme
½ teaspoon dried fenugreek/ methi leaves
3 cardamom pods
1 teaspoon paprika
1 teaspoon salt
3 garlic cloves, chopped
400g canned chopped tomatoes
250ml beef stock (see page 17)
100g chestnut mushrooms, halved

For the raita
Half a cucumber, diced
½ teaspoon salt
150ml plain yoghurt
1 tablespoon fresh mint, chopped finely

1. Preheat the oven to 180°C/gas mark 4.

2. Melt the butter in a large pan or lidded casserole and fry the onions and peppers very gently for 3 minutes.

3. Add the meat and all the spices, herbs and seasoning and stir well so that the meat is thoroughly coated.

4. Stir in the garlic and add the tomatoes and stock. Put on the lid and cook in the oven for 1 hour. Add the mushrooms and stir.

5. Cover and turn down the heat to 160°C/gas 2–3 and cook for 1½ hours. Check the liquid content halfway through cooking time and stir in a little more hot water if necessary.

6. Serve with the raita (below), and pilau rice, naan bread (see page 113) and mango chutney (see page 195).

For the raita
1. Put the cucumber in a colander over a bowl and sprinkle with the salt. Leave for 30 minutes.

2. Put the yoghurt in a bowl and mix in the mint and cucumber.

3. Decorate with a few mint leaves and place in the fridge to chill before serving.

Tiramisu

SERVES 6

100ml single cream
3 egg yolks
500g mascarpone cheese
3 rounded tablespoons caster sugar
350ml very strong coffee (at least twice the strength of normal)
50ml brandy
20–22 ratafia biscuits
1 heaped tablespoon cocoa

1. Beat the cream and egg yolks into the mascarpone.

2. Beat in the sugar.

3. Combine the coffee and brandy in a bowl and dip the biscuits in one by one. Lay them in a serving dish close together.

4. When the base is covered, spread half of the cheese mixture over the biscuits and repeat the process.

5. Sieve the cocoa over the top of the tiramisu very generously. Leave to set for at least an hour before serving.

Chocolate Orange Mousse

SERVES 6

300g dark chocolate
25g unsalted butter
5 eggs
80g golden caster sugar
Zest and juice of 1 orange
250ml whipping cream, whipped to form soft peaks
1 tablespoon Grand Marnier or Cointreau

1. Reserve 2 pieces of the chocolate and melt the rest with the butter in a bowl over a pan of hot water.

2. Whisk the eggs, sugar, orange zest and juice together until light and fluffy.

3. Whisk the eggs into the chocolate and fold in the cream and the liqueur.

4. Spoon into ramekins and decorate with a little grated chocolate shaved from the 2 reserved pieces.

5. Chill before serving.

Summer Fruit Pudding

This is best made the night or day before serving, so is ideal to serve at a special meal.

- 8–9 slices thick white bread, crusts removed
- 750–800g mixed fruit: strawberries, pitted cherries, blackcurrants, raspberries and blueberries
- 75g caster sugar

1. Cut a circle of bread to fit the base of a 1.2-litre bowl or pudding basin exactly.

2. Line the rest of the basin with the other slices, overlapping them so that some of the bread sits above the bowl's rim.

3. Put the fruit in a large saucepan along with the sugar and heat gently until all the sugar has dissolved. Simmer for 5 minutes until all the juices of the fruit begin to run freely. Allow to cool.

4. Spoon the fruit into the bread-lined bowl and fold over the top edges.

5. Make a 'lid' for the top of the pudding with another bread slice and press down gently with your hand. Put a saucer or plate over the top (one that fits inside the bowl). Place a weight or heavy tin on top and chill in the fridge for at least 8 hours.

6. Serve with crème fraîche or cream.

Spiced Pears with Ginger Cream

- 6 ripe pears
- Juice and grated rind of 1 lemon
- 350ml water
- 120g golden caster sugar
- 2 cloves
- 1 small cinnamon stick
- A little grated nutmeg

For the cream

- 200ml double cream
- 1 dessertspoon icing sugar
- ½ level teaspoon of freshly grated ginger

1. Peel the pears, halve them and remove the cores. Squeeze the lemon juice over them.

2. Put the water, lemon rind, sugar and spices into a saucepan over a medium heat. Stir until the sugar has dissolved.

3. Put the pears in the syrup, bring to the boil, then turn down the heat and simmer very gently for 6–8 minutes. The pears should be just tender.

4. Leave to cool in the syrup before dividing into dessert bowls.

5. Whip the cream and sugar together until thickened slightly and stir in the ginger.

6. Serve with the pears.

My Notes

15

Bread and Scones

Bread-making is one of the most satisfying things I know. Even after 30 years of home bread-making, I still experience the sense of pride when I lift a loaf out of the oven. And it doesn't stop there. When people eat it and say how good it is, it is a thrill to know it is my own creation.

My neighbours recently told me that they have to shut their windows when I'm bread-making because it always makes them hungry. It certainly has that effect on my family. When there is bread in the oven, you can't get them out of the kitchen; they are always raiding the fridge! The aroma of warm bread is probably the best way of making a house seem homely and lived in, so forget all your air fresheners – bake some bread! It is so simple to make these days, and if you use the fast-action-type yeast, it is also much quicker than it used to be.

TIPS AND TECHNIQUES

Bread-making Essentials

You will need the following utensils to hand when you begin making your own bread:

- A large mixing bowl, either ceramic or plastic. A ceramic bowl is more stable, but it is heavier, so bear in mind that you'll need to move it around when it's filled with heavy dough.
- A couple of large baking sheets
- 1or 2 x 450g/1lb loaf tins
- An oven that reaches at least 220°C/gas mark 7

Remember to remove your rings or any jewellery when making bread by hand. This is for the sake of hygiene as well as for the preservation of your jewellery.

Types of flour

Many recipes that call for white flour, such as the one on the next page, can also be made using brown or wholemeal flour. But remember: wholemeal flour will need more liquid than white flour, so you will have to use more water. Also bear in mind that wholemeal flour is heavier than white, so it will yield a denser, weightier loaf.

Know your oven

If you find that your loaves brown too quickly on the top, lower their position in the oven. Likewise, if they're browning too quickly on the base, raise their oven position. You might not be aware of this until after you've made your first batch of bread, because every oven is different, but you'll soon get to know the best baking position. Remember, the first few loaves won't necessarily be perfect. The important thing is just to have a go.

The 'tap test'

The traditional method of testing whether your bread has baked completely is the 'tap test'. Remove a loaf from its pan and rap the base sharply with your knuckles. If the loaf is cooked through it should make a hollow sound. If not, then it needs more time in the oven.

Resist temptation!

Never slice a loaf that has just come out of the oven, no matter how tempting it smells. It will lose its shape and texture when squashed with the pressure of cutting. Leave it for at least 40 minutes whenever possible. It will still be warm but much easier to cut.

MAKES 2 X 450G/1LB LOAVES OR 12 INDIVIDUAL ROLLS

Simple White Loaf

This is a good place to begin if you've never cooked with yeast before. Don't worry about making mistakes – everybody does. But do give it a try: it is well worth the effort.

- 900g strong white flour
- 2 level teaspoons salt
- 1 x 7g sachet fast-action dried yeast
- 450ml warm water
- 1 tablespoon sunflower or olive oil
- Oil for greasing

1. Sieve the flour and salt together into a mixing bowl. Stir in the yeast.

2. Make a well in the centre of the flour and add half of the water, then the oil. Stir in with a wooden spoon.

3. Add a little more water at a time and keep mixing. When you have added all the water, use your hands to bring the dough together. It should feel moist; if not, add more water. The dough must be moist to rise well.

4. Really work the dough with your hands until it is well combined and begins to form a smooth dough.

5. Flour a work surface and knead the dough for 10 minutes. This process will make the finished loaf light and soft, so be vigorous.

6. Divide and shape the dough into any shape you like and place in lightly oiled loaf tins or on a baking sheet. Cover with a clean tea towel and leave in a warm place to 'prove' (rise) until doubled in size. This will take between 35–45 minutes. About 15–20 minutes after proving time has begun, preheat the oven to 220°C/gas mark 7.

7. Bake small rolls for 15–20 minutes, large loaves for 30-40 minutes. If the large loaves begin to brown after 20 minutes, turn down the heat to 200°C/gas mark 6 for the rest of the baking time.

8. Perform the 'tap test' to see if the bread is done (see page 242).

9. Take the bread out of the tin immediately as otherwise it will lose its crustiness. Cool on a wire rack for at least 40 minutes before slicing.

Granary Bread

MAKES 2 LOAVES

- 600g strong white or brown flour
- 2 level teaspoons salt
- 300g granary flour
- 1 x 7g sachet fast-action dried yeast
- 568ml warm water
- 1 tablespoon sunflower or olive oil, plus extra for greasing

1. Sieve the white or brown flour and salt together into a mixing bowl and stir in the granary flour and yeast.

2. Make a well in the centre and add half of the water, then the oil. Mix and add the rest of the water.

3. Mix with your hands to combine all the ingredients and form a dough.

4. Transfer to a lightly floured surface and knead vigorously for 10 minutes.

5. Shape into two round cobs and place on a baking sheet, or put into 2 lightly oiled loaf tins. Leave to prove for 35–45 minutes, or until doubled in size.

6. Bake at 220°C/gas mark 7 for 30–40 minutes, or until deep golden-brown on top.

7. Perform the 'tap test' to see if the bread is done (see page 242).

8. Transfer to a wire rack and allow to cool completely.

Oatmeal Bread

MAKES 2 LOAVES

- 700g strong white flour
- 2 teaspoons salt
- 200g porridge oats
- 1x 7g sachet fast-action dried yeast
- 480ml warm water
- 1 tablespoon sunflower or olive oil, plus extra for greasing

1. Sieve the flour and salt together in a mixing bowl and stir in the oats. Make a well in the centre and add half of the water, then the oil. Mix, then add the rest of the water.

2. Use your hands to combine all the ingredients and form a dough.

3. Transfer to a lightly floured surface and knead vigorously for 10 minutes.

4. Shape into two round cobs and place on a baking sheet, or put into 2 lightly oiled loaf tins. Leave to prove for 35–45 minutes, or until doubled in size.

5. Bake at 220°C/gas mark 7 for 30–40 minutes, or until deep golden-brown on top.

6. Perform the 'tap test' to see if the bread is done (see page 242).

7. Transfer to a wire rack and allow to cool completely.

MAKES 1 LARGE LOAF

Onion Bread

- 50g butter
- 2 small onions, finely sliced
- ½ teaspoon salt
- 500g strong white flour
- 2 teaspoons salt
- 1 x 7g sachet fast-action dried yeast
- 1 tablespoon onion seeds
- 300ml warm water
- 1 tablespoon sunflower or olive oil, plus extra for greasing
- Onion seeds for sprinkling on the top

1. Heat the butter in a saucepan and fry the onions gently until they begin to caramelise. Sprinkle in the salt. Finish caramelising the onions, transfer to a dish and leave to cool.

2. Sieve the flour and salt together into a mixing bowl. Stir in the yeast and onion seeds.

3. Make a well in the centre of the flour and add half of the water, then the oil. Stir in with a wooden spoon.

4. Add a little more water at a time and keep mixing. When you have added all the water, use your hands to bring the dough together. It should feel moist; if not, add more water. The dough must be moist to rise well.

5. Really work the dough with your hands until it is well combined and begins to form a smooth dough.

6. Flour a work surface and knead the dough for 10 minutes. This process will make the finished loaf light and soft, so be vigorous.

7. Shape the dough into 1 large loaf and place on a lightly oiled baking sheet. Cover with a clean tea towel and leave in a warm place to 'prove' (rise) until doubled in size. This will take between 35–45 minutes. After about 30 minutes into the proving time, spread the caramelised onions over the top, pressing them lightly into the surface, then sprinkle with some extra onion seed. About 15–20 minutes after proving time has begun, preheat the oven to 220°C/gas mark 7.

8. Bake for 15 minutes at 220°C/gas mark 7, then turn down the heat to 200°C/gas mark 6 and bake for 15–20 minutes longer.

9. Perform the 'tap test' to see if the bread is done (see page 242), then transfer to a wire rack to cool.

BREAKFAST TIME

MAKES 8

Breakfast Muffins

280g strong white flour
1 level teaspoon salt
Half a 7g sachet fast-action dried yeast
220ml warm water
Oil for greasing

1. Sieve the flour and salt together. Stir in the yeast.

2. Make a well in the flour and stir in enough water until a soft dough is formed.

3. Knead the dough for 8–10 minutes until it is smooth.

4. Leave to prove for 40 minutes in a warm place.

5. When the dough has doubled in size, break off small, even quantities and form into rounds; do this lightly so as to conserve the lightness of the dough.

6. Heat a griddle pan or large flat-based frying pan that has been lightly oiled and cook the muffins 3–4 at a time. Keep the pan on a medium heat or they will burn. Cook for 5 minutes each side, and keep the cooked ones warm in the oven until all are done. Alternatively, allow them to cool and toast when required.

BREAKFAST TIME

Crumpets

I find it better to use fresh yeast or ordinary dried yeast in this recipe because the yeast needs time to ferment to allow the bubbles of air to form.

220g strong white flour
1 level teaspoon salt
150ml warm milk
150ml warm water
15g fresh or dried yeast
½ teaspoon sugar
½ teaspoon baking soda
4 tablespoons cold water
1 egg white, whisked until frothy
Oil for greasing

1. Sieve together the flour and the salt into a large bowl.

2. In another bowl, mix the milk and warm water together, crumble in the fresh yeast or stir in the dried yeast. Add the sugar and stir.

3. Pour the yeast mixture into the flour and beat vigorously for 3–4 minutes. Leave it in a warm place covered with a tea towel for 30 minutes.

4. Stir the baking soda into the cold water and add to the yeast mixture. Fold in the egg white. Make sure everything is thoroughly combined.

5. Heat a lightly oiled griddle until hot and use oiled food rings to form the crumpets on the griddle. Ladle the mixture into each ring and cook until the crumpet looks set on the top. This will take about 4–5 minutes.

6. Carefully remove the rings from the crumpets and put on wire racks to cool. Do this until all the mixture is used up. Serve toasted with butter.

Variation
You can make pikelets with this mixture instead of crumpets; they are easier but much flatter. Simply ladle small amounts of the mixture straight onto the griddle without the rings and cook for 3 minutes each side, or until golden.

SWEETENED BREAD

MAKES 3 SMALL LOAVES OR 8 INDIVIDUAL ROLLS

Sally Lunn Loaves

A rich bread that tastes good at breakfast, teatime or supper.

380g strong white flour
½ teaspoon salt
1 x 7g sachet fast-action dried yeast
40g caster sugar
1 large egg, beaten
Finely grated rind of 1 lemon
150ml warm water
50g butter, melted
Oil for greasing

1. Sieve the flour and salt together and stir in the yeast and sugar.

2. Make a well in the centre of the flour and add the egg and lemon rind. Stir into the flour.

3. Stir in the water and mix thoroughly. Pour in the melted butter and mix.

4. Knead the dough until smooth, then transfer to a lightly floured surface.

5. Divide the mixture into 3 sections and knead each for 3–4 minutes. Place on an oiled baking sheet and leave to prove for 30 minutes in a warm place.

6. Just before baking, brush the tops with a little beaten egg. Bake for 15–20 minutes at 220°C/gas mark 7.

Fruited Teacakes

MAKES 10–12

450g strong white flour
1 level teaspoon salt
1 x 7g sachet fast-action dried yeast
50g caster sugar
40g softened butter
300ml warm milk
50g currants
50g sultanas
25g mixed peel
Oil for greasing

1. Sieve the flour and salt together and stir in the yeast and sugar.

2. Rub in the butter.

3. Make a well in the centre and pour in the milk. Stir and mix with your hands to combine.

4. Knead to form a dough, then add the fruit. Knead this all in and continue to knead for 3–4 minutes.

5. Break off equal amounts of the dough, roll into balls and place on an oiled baking sheet. Press down the balls to make flat discs.

6. Leave to prove for 30 minutes, then bake at 220°C/gas mark 7 for 10–15 minutes.

Variation
The fruit may be omitted if you prefer a plain teacake.

MAKES 8 LARGE SLICES

Marmalade Tea Bread

This is more of a cake, really, as it doesn't contain yeast. It is wonderful served with a cup of tea in the afternoon.

- Butter for greasing
- 200g self-raising flour
- 1 teaspoon cinnamon
- 60g muscovado sugar
- 100g butter
- 1 egg, beaten
- 5 tablespoons milk
- 3 tablespoons marmalade

1. Preheat the oven to 160°C/gas mark 2–3. Grease a loaf tin.
2. Sieve the flour and cinnamon into a mixing bowl and stir in the sugar.
3. Rub the butter into the flour mixture until it resembles breadcrumbs.
4. In a separate bowl or jug, beat the egg into the milk and stir in the marmalade. Pour this into the flour mixture and beat well with a wooden spoon.
5. Spoon the mixture into the loaf tin and bake for 50–60 minutes until deep golden in colour.
6. Brush the top with marmalade. Allow to cool for 15 minutes before removing from the tin. Cool on a wire rack.

Millie's Easy Bran Loaf

I use a medium-sized coffee mug to measure my ingredients for this recipe. If you don't like it too sweet, simply use less sugar.

- 1 mug mixed raisins and sultanas
- 1 mug All Bran cereal
- 1 mug cold strong tea
- 1 mug self-raising flour
- 1 mug brown sugar
- 5 tablespoons milk

1. Mix the fruit and All Bran together in a mixing bowl. Pour in the tea. Leave for 6–8 hours or overnight.
2. Stir in the flour, sugar and milk and combine well. If the mixture looks too dry, add another tablespoonful of milk.
3. Pour into a buttered loaf tin and bake at 180°C/gas mark 4 for 1¼ hours.
4. Leave in the tin for 10 minutes before transferring to a wire rack to cool.
5. When cool, wrap in greaseproof paper and leave to mature for 24 hours.

MAKES 2 SMALL LOAVES

Malt Loaf

Butter for greasing
220g self-raising flour
220g sultanas
170g malt extract
1 tablespoon black treacle
50g muscovado sugar
2 eggs
150ml tea

1. Preheat the oven to 160°C/gas mark 2–3. Butter 2 loaf tins.

2. Sieve the flour into a bowl and stir in the fruit.

3. Heat the malt extract, treacle and sugar in a saucepan over a low heat, then pour over the fruit and flour. Stir to combine.

4. Add the eggs and tea and beat the mixture well until smooth.

5. Spoon into the tins and bake for 1 hour until springy to the touch.

6. Leave in the tins for 10 minutes before transferring the loaves to a wire rack to cool.

MAKES 20 LARGE SCONES

Plain Scones

These go so well with cream and jam.

- Butter for greasing
- 1 tablespoon lemon juice
- 380ml milk
- 450g self-raising flour
- 2 tablespoons golden caster sugar
- 60g butter, chopped into small pieces

1. Preheat the oven to 200°C/gas mark 6. Grease 2 baking sheets.

2. Mix the lemon juice in the milk and stir. Leave for 5 minutes while you weigh out your ingredients. This acidified milk helps lighten the scones.

3. Sieve the flour into a bowl and stir in the sugar.

4. Add the butter and rub into the flour until it looks like breadcrumbs. Mix in the milk with quick light strokes until well combined.

5. Bring the mixture together with your hands. Knead as lightly as possible until the dough is pliable.

6. Roll out half the dough to about 2.5cm thick and cut into rounds.

7. Place on a baking sheet and do the same with the other half of the dough. Rolling in two batches like this stops the dough from getting tough after being re-rolled.

8. Bake for 20 minutes until well risen and golden brown.

9. Allow to cool for 10 minutes to help with the slicing. Serve hot or cold.

Variation
To make a fruited version, simply add 60g sultanas and/or raisins to the scone mixture just after rubbing in the butter.

SCONES

Cheese Scones

Butter for greasing
250g self-raising flour
1 level teaspoon salt
½ level teaspoon mustard powder
80g mature Cheddar, grated
Black pepper to taste
1 egg
180ml milk with 1 tablespoon lemon juice stirred in

1. Preheat the oven to 220°C/gas mark 7. Grease a baking sheet.

2. Sieve the flour, salt and mustard together in a mixing bowl.

3. Stir in half of the cheese and season with black pepper.

4. Beat the egg into the milk and pour into the flour. Mix the liquid into the flour and combine well.

5. Use your hands to knead the dough very lightly and form it into a ball.

6. Place the dough on the baking sheet and press gently down with your hands to form a large round about 2cm deep.

7. Sprinkle the top with the rest of the cheese and bake for 20 minutes until well risen and golden. Cut into 6–8 portions when cool. Serve cut in half and buttered.

Variations
Use other ingredients to vary the flavour:

- 1 teaspoon of paprika instead of mustard and 25g of finely chopped chorizo sausage
- 1 teaspoon mixed herbs
- 30g chopped sun-dried tomatoes
- 25g chopped black olives and Parmesan instead of Cheddar

My Notes

16

Making Your Own Bacon and Sausages

My son Joshua loves homemade bacon because of the flavour. My daughter, Rebecca, loves it because it is healthy and 'low salt'. I love it because Paul can eat it and it doesn't bother his blood pressure. I also love it because it is a complete thrill to make. Who would have thought of making bacon – *your own bacon* – at home in the kitchen? All the utensils you need are at hand: a tray, a dish and a spoon. Besides the meat, you only need two ingredients: sugar and salt.

Making sausage is much the same, but more fun. I guarantee that you will not be able to load a sausage skin onto a nozzle without at least a little smile – unless, like me, you simply fall about laughing!

BACON

Making Pork into Bacon

Why should I make my own bacon?

Firstly, it costs much less than commercially produced bacon. Secondly, it has much less salt and no saltpetre or nitrite, which is what preserves bacon and gives it that pink colour. Yet there is no reason why bacon *has* to be pink; the colour doesn't affect the flavour. And when you make your own, you won't keep it around long enough for it to need preservatives!

What do I need?

Besides a large baking tray for preparing the bacon, there are only three ingredients.

Loin and lean belly pork are the best cuts for making bacon. Ask your butcher to slice the meat like bacon for you, as this is easier than doing it yourself. If you want to do it yourself, however, use a large, very sharp knife, or a meat slicer if you have one.

Sugar is part of the curing process and enhances the flavour of the finished bacon. Use the same amount of sugar as salt to make your cure. Mix it together in a small bowl.

Salt is the only other ingredient. Use it in the following quantities.

- 1 teaspoon or 5g per kilo of meat gives very mild bacon
- 2 teaspoons or 10g per kilo gives a stronger flavour and is my favourite
- 3 teaspoons or 15g per kilo gives a stronger flavour still, but it uses only half the salt content of commercial bacon

How do I make the pork into bacon?

1. Make your chosen quantity of cure.
2. Lay the slices of pork on a baking tray.
3. Sprinkle the cure over the lean meat only. Tiny amounts are sufficient.
4. Lay one piece on top of the other, so that the cure reaches both sides. Remember to do the underside of the bottom layer.
5. Place in the fridge, uncovered, overnight. You will have bacon in the morning! The meat will have given off a pink liquor; this shows the cure is working.
6. Cook as you would ordinary bacon, but don't use high heat because this will make it tough. This is true with most bacon – not just home-cured.
7. Once cured, keep in the fridge and eat within 4 days, or freeze in batches.

SAUSAGES

Making Sausages

What will I need?

Besides a large mixing bowl, you will need the following to make sausages at home.

- *A sausage stuffer.* Some food processors come with these as an extra attachment. If you haven't got one, you can buy a hand-cranked mincing machine. They do the job quite slowly, but you have more control over the flow of meat.
- *Casings.* These can be purchased from sausage-making companies. Some butchers will also sell you some. Always read the instructions, as they have to be soaked in water before use. Hog casings are best; they have the least smell and are strong enough to withstand the handling. You can buy cellulose and halal ones, too.
- *Minced meat.* Most meat can be turned into sausages. You'll need to add some fat as this is what helps cook the sausage from the inside. It also produces a better-tasting, more tender sausage.
- *Breadcrumbs.* An important ingredient: it binds the ingredients and soaks up the juices of the meat, which gives the sausage a good consistency.
- *Seasoning.* This can be salt, herbs or spices. The best thing is that you control exactly how much salt they contain.
- *Flavourings.* Apple, onion, sun-dried tomato… the list is endless, and the choice is entirely up to you.
- *Water.* Without it, stuffing the sausage would be impossible. It also helps keep the sausage moist and juicy.

The Basic Sausage Recipe

1kg pork shoulder steak, minced, or buy minced pork for ease at first
200g breadcrumbs
200ml water
1 teaspoon salt
½ teaspoon black pepper

1. Combine all the ingredients in a large bowl. It is very important to mix them well in order to give an even flavour. Use your hands for best results.

2. Keep your hands wet when pushing the casing onto the stuffing tube. Don't use too much; making batches of sausage is the easiest. Two people at this stage are better than one – and it is much more fun!

3. Turn the handle of the stuffer slowly and smoothly, and have someone catch the sausages at the other end to keep them moving evenly. Don't overfill the casing or it will pop when cooking. Don't attempt to link your sausages until all the meat has been used up. If a casing bursts (and it will), just pull it gently and keep filling.

4. Twist the sausage at regular intervals to make links. You can make them as long or as short as you wish. These will freeze well and keep for 36–48 hours in the fridge.

Variations
Use the basic recipe for all the variations below, but add:

Paprika Pork
10g paprika
4 garlic cloves, grated

Sun-dried Tomato
100g sun-dried tomatoes in oil, finely chopped
2 tablespoons of the oil the tomatoes are in
2 teaspoons caster sugar

Lincolnshire-style
15g sage (dried is best)
10g ground black pepper

Cumberland-style
10g ground black pepper
5g grated nutmeg
½ teaspoon dried sage

SAUSAGES

Pork and Apple

1kg pork, minced
3 Granny Smith apples, peeled; grate 2 and chop 1 into small cubes
80g breadcrumbs
120ml apple juice
10g salt
½ teaspoon black pepper
15g dried thyme

1. Combine all the ingredients in a large bowl, then follow the steps in the Basic Sausage recipe.

Beef Sausage

1kg shoulder steak, minced
250g beef suet
250g breadcrumbs
200g water
1 teaspoon salt
½ teaspoon white pepper

For spicy beef sausage, add
10g mustard powder
½ teaspoon ground coriander
1 teaspoon ground cumin
½ teaspoon ground ginger

1. Combine all the ingredients in a large bowl, then follow the steps in the Basic Sausage recipe.

Turkey Sausage

1kg turkey meat
100g pork fat
150g fine oats
150g water
15g salt
½ teaspoon pepper

1. Grind the meat and fat together and combine in a mixing bowl with all the other ingredients.

2. Stuff the sausage as before, but leave overnight in the fridge before cooking or freezing.

My Notes

Index

T

V

W

Y

Z